photo by Howard Sochurek

URBAN
DESIGN
MANHATTAN

Stanley B. Tankel, Planning Director of Regional Plan Association from July 1, 1960 to his untimely death, March 31, 1968, led in the conception of the broad outlines of the Second Regional Plan.

A major recommendation of the Plan is the reinforcement of existing and the creation of new urban centers throughout the Region. The center of centers—Manhattan—needs planning and design attention commensurate with its scale. Mr. Tankel commissioned this study, contributed to the development of its principles, and played an important part in organizing its presentation both as an exhibition at the Architectural League in February 1968 and in this publication, which he began editing before his death.

The officers, directors, members and staff of the Association appreciate Mr. Tankel's profound contribution to the New York Metropolitan Region, which he deeply loved.

A REPORT OF THE SECOND REGIONAL PLAN, APRIL, 1969

Manhattan — 1963

URBAN DESIGN MANHATTAN

REGIONAL PLAN ASSOCIATION

Prepared by Rai Y. Okamoto and Frank E. Williams,
Urban Design Consultants, with Klaus Huboi.
Assisted by Dietrich Kunkel and Carlisle Towery.
Chapter 5 prepared by C. McKim Norton. Edited by
Stanley B. Tankel, Boris Pushkarev and William B. Shore.
Graphic organization and design by Barbara Towery.

A STUDIO BOOK · THE VIKING PRESS · NEW YORK

Second Regional Plan publications

The Region's Growth (May 1967)
Projections of jobs by type, population, households and income for the New York Metropolitan Region, 1965-2000, with a section on world urbanization and the Atlantic Urban Region.

Public Participation in Regional Planning
(October 1967)
The importance and difficulties of involving the public in planning, and results of RPA's pioneering 1963 Goals Project.

Jamaica Center (April 1968)
Prototype study of a major urban center: the possibilities, design, transportation and process of developing Jamaica, Queens, with a summary of arguments for large centers, particularly in the old Core of the Region.

The Lower Hudson (December 1966)
The potential of the Hudson River Valley below the George Washington Bridge as a public amenity — one example of how to meet the conflict between preserving nature and the growth of a metropolis.

Waste Management (March 1968)
How to organize a metropolitan area for efficient waste management: what information is needed, where controls can be applied, how to project waste generation of the future and how the pattern of urbanization affects waste generation and handling.

Public Services in Older Cities (May 1968)
Costs of public services needed to break the cycle of poverty and improve living conditions for all income groups in older cities, with recommendations for financing them.

Copyright © 1969 by Regional Plan Association, Inc.
230 West 41st Street, New York, N.Y. 10036
All rights reserved

First published in 1969 by The Viking Press, Inc.
625 Madison Avenue, New York, N.Y. 10022

Published simultaneously in Canada by
The Macmillan Company of Canada Limited

Library of Congress catalog card number: 69-17969

Printed in U.S.A.

CONTENTS

FOREWORD

This book was written in response to questions which arose in the course of our work on the future of the New York Metropolitan Region when it became clear that employment in office buildings probably would double in about thirty-five years.

If offices are built at that pace, we asked the authors, can they be designed and located so they provide an efficient and enjoyable environment for office workers? Particularly, can this be achieved in a central business district like mid-Manhattan for which there is no plan other than its existing street and subway lines and economic compulsions as molded by the municipal Zoning Resolution? Are there better design principles than those which today produce nearly uniform office buildings running in slab formation like dominos up midtown avenues? Must the journey from subway door to office elevator be an increasingly degrading shuffle on crowded stairs and along sordid underground pedestrian ways? Can the City accommodate great new office buildings without losing services and amenities that make the City an exciting working environment, such as those provided today — but fast vanishing — in specialty shops, small restaurants, personal service establishments and the multitude of unexpected elements that comprise the sidewalk scene? Can we handle increased crowds of workers, shoppers, theatre goers and holiday makers? Can we give the walker or driver in the City a sense of place such as one experiences on reaching Rockefeller Center and misses on Third Avenue's midtown blocks?

A special design staff collaborated with Regional Plan Association's regular professional staff in city planning, urban economics, public administration and law to answer these and related questions in this book. Advice was also sought from an urban sociologist and a psychologist who headed a separate study on the effects of crowding on human behavior.

Urban Design Manhattan recommends principles to guide the growth of a high density central business district. While midtown Manhattan, the area selected for testing the design principles, is unique in many respects, the approach to problems and opportunities there is applicable to other cities throughout the world looking forward to central business district growth.

The study shows that a large and dense center does not have to be chaotic, overcrowded and dingy. It conceives of all the facilities for urban movement — the trains and subways, the sidewalks, the building lobbies and elevators — as a single system, a structure to which individual buildings are attached. It proposes to break through the "asphalt membrane" which now divides the city into "above ground" and "underground," to unify the circulation spaces functionally and visually, creating a true three-dimensional city. The study also suggests legal and administrative measures which could help implement the concepts proposed.

In 1968, the main elements of this book were presented as exhibits sponsored in New York City by the Architectural League of New York, in Philadelphia by the International Federation of Housing and Planning, at Milan's Triennale and on a Smithsonian national tour.

Urban Design Manhattan is the seventh in a series of reports leading to the Second Regional Plan for the New York Metropolitan Region, sequel to the **Regional Plan of New York and Its Environs** of 1929.

Like its predecessor, the Second Regional Plan comprises a set of compatible recommendations to guide the development patterns for the anticipated population and economic growth and the resulting environmental quality.

Two reports on environmental quality preceded this volume: **The Lower Hudson** (1966), which suggested urban design principles to harmonize man-made development with natural beauty, and **Waste Management** (1968), which deals with the handling of man-made wastes in the context of the Region's land, air and water resources.

The estimates of increase in office employment in mid-Manhattan used in this report are based on economic and demographic projections reported in **The Region's Growth** (1967) and expanded in a forthcoming study of office location; the transportation assumptions are based on work in progress for a forthcoming Second Regional Plan report, **Regional Transportation.**

Regional Plan Association, an unofficial citizens group organized in 1929 to foster and develop the first Regional Plan, continues to pursue the goal of improving the living conditions for the people of the tri-state Region surrounding the Port of New York.

Second Regional Plan research, of which this report is a part, is being financed by the Avalon, Ford, Rockefeller Brothers and Taconic foundations. Other stages of Association work leading to the Second Plan were also financed by these foundations and the Merrill, New York, Twentieth Century, Victoria and Old Dominion foundations.

In the period 1957-1968 during which this work was conducted, the Association was led by Harold S. Osborne, Amory H. Bradford, James S. Schoff and Max Abramovitz. Each has contributed significantly to the making of the Second Regional Plan.

This publication has been reviewed and accepted for publication by Regional Plan's Board of Directors.

C. McKim Norton
President

5

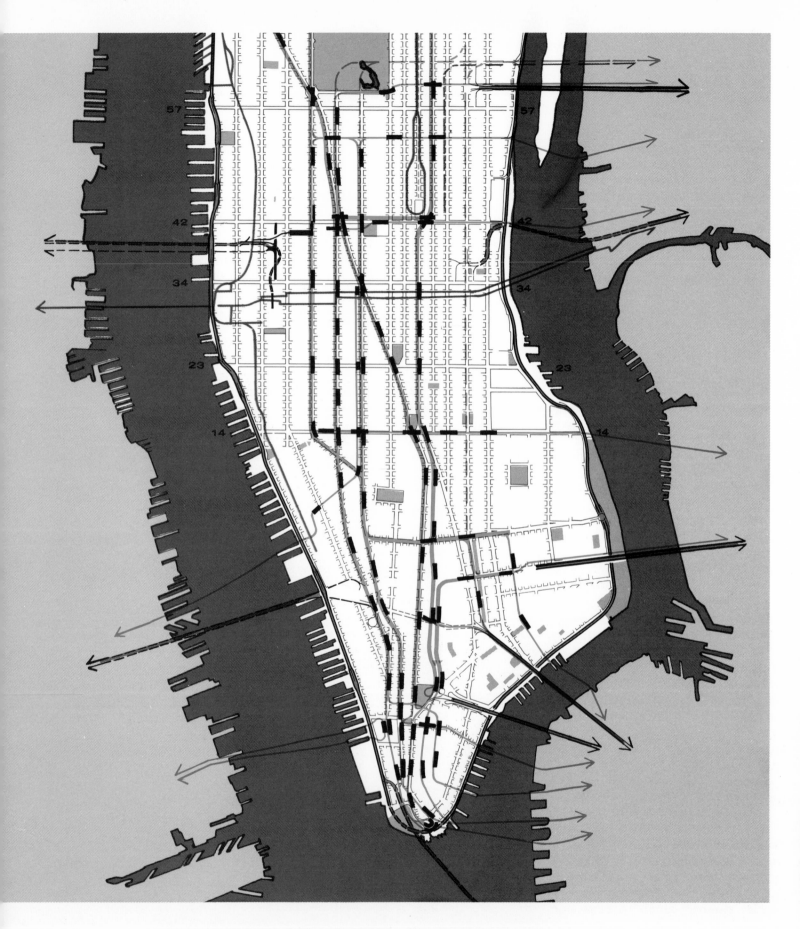

The Central Business District of Manhattan (CBD) is the 8.6 square miles south of 61st Street bounded by Central Park, the two rivers and the harbor. 800 million square feet of building floorspace —close to one tenth of the Region's total, including 540 million square feet of non-residential floorspace, or one sixth of the Region's total, are located in this .07 percent of its area. The orientation map at left shows the grid of principal transportation arteries — the 40 tracks of subways, 10 tracks of railroads, .62 lanes of expressways, bridges and tunnels, and 87 lanes of arterial streets which daily carry 3.3 million people into the CBD. Organizing a pleasant and efficient circulation for these people once they become pedestrians in the CBD is one of the key objectives of this publication.

— limited access highways, tunnels and bridges

■ regional, commuter, freight and service rail

■ metropolitan subway

■ subway stations

■ major public parks

INTRODUCTION AND SUMMARY

Clustering those urban activities that can profit from concentration in large centers is a key policy of The Second Regional Plan for the New York Region. A corollary of this policy is to facilitate, rather than inhibit, location of urban activities in the Region's largest center, the central business district (CBD) in Manhattan south of Central Park. This volume, therefore, is one of a series of back-up reports for the Plan.

Facilitating added activities in the Manhattan CBD requires unusual attention to planning and design. This is the most intensively used land in the world, with values of $200 a square foot common, and $500 a square foot not unusual. While the 550,000 residents of the CBD constitute but 3 percent of the Region's 19 million population, it has 2 million jobs — 26 percent of the Region's total.

Nevertheless, design principles so essential to efficiency and amenity in the Manhattan CBD are equally applicable in any larger cluster of urban activities. Manhattan's size and complexity simply make the importance of the principles more apparent.

Unfortunately, Manhattan has not had a plan — except in fractional ways — since 1811, when the basic grid of streets and avenues was laid out. A useful plan for growth and change in an area where a typical office building costs $25-50 million, and two subway tracks — over $30 million a mile would require the continuing effort of a large, full time staff, funded commeasurately with its task, collaborating closely with a number of public and private agencies. This report can only indicate what some concerns of that staff should be.

The report's emphasis is on qualitative aspects of visual and functional organization, hence the title "Urban Design." Some of the quantitative aspects, as well as Manhattan's relationship to the rest of the Region, will be covered more fully in subsequent reports on regional activities and on transportation.

Dimensions and Growth of the Manhattan Central Business District

Manhattan south of Central Park covers .07 percent of the Region's geographic area; yet, 9 percent — 130 times

the share — of the Region's building space is clustered on this land, some 800 million square feet. Among other measures of the CBD's prominence are:

1. **The high income of its workers.** Forty percent of the workers with annual incomes over $10,000 worked in the CBD in 1960, compared to 26 percent of all workers in the 31-county Study Area for The Second Regional Plan.

2. **The powerful influence it exerts on the Region's transportation network.** About 20 percent of all non-pedestrian trips in the Region are to or from the CBD. Because of their length, they account for nearly 30 percent of all person-miles of travel. Two-thirds of public transit person-miles of travel occur on trips to and from the CBD, and 49 percent of the Region's air trips are made by people who leave for the airport from there.

3. **Its concentration of special activities.** The CBD contains 52 percent of the Region's jobs in office buildings, 76 percent of its legitimate theatres, 26 percent of department store floor space, 25 percent of manufacturing/warehousing employment, and 14 percent of college enrollment.

The most dynamic factor in the future of the central business district will be the growth of jobs in office buildings. Jobs in office buildings in the entire 31-county Study Area are expected to nearly double over the rest of the century, and about one-third of the projected increase — some 500,000 office jobs — can be expected, by their type, to be located in the CBD if conditions allow it. Taking into account substantial declines in factory and warehousing jobs and some increase in service jobs, a net increase in total CBD employment from some 2.1 million to over 2.4 million in the year 2000 can be foreseen.

To accommodate the projected growth in office jobs, more than 100 million square feet of rentable office floor space will have to be built, in addition to an estimated 75 million square feet for the replacement of obsolete structures. Huge as these projections are, they are not out of line with past performance: in the 1950-59 decade, 32 million square feet, and in 1960-69, 55 million square feet of rental space in commercial office buildings was built in the Manhattan central business district.

Despite the confined area of the CBD, the land requirement for this added construction is not a serious constraint. Currently, office buildings occupy only 5 percent of the central business district's land area, or about 250 acres. An additional 100 million square feet would cover less than 200 acres. More land than that is likely to become available over the same period due to the decline in manufacturing activity alone.

In fact, the primary concern of this report is that the new buildings will spill over too wide an area. Densities even higher than those presently encountered in Manhattan can be comfortable, without congestion, if the pedestrian circulation areas are deliberately dimensioned to accommodate the person-miles of pedestrian movement that activities in the buildings generate. Yet, traffic engineering for the pedestrian has been rare and standards low. Even factual data on trip generation and comfortable densities of pedestrian movement is sparse.

The major constraint is not space in the CBD but the delivery capacity and the tributary area of the hub-bound transportation systems. They have been essentially stable for four decades, a fact not unrelated to the stability of total employment in Manhattan over the same period. (Thirty-four lanes of limited-access highways, bridges, and tunnels were added between 1932 and 1958 for automobiles and buses, but they carry only 10 percent of the peak-hour person-trips into and out of the CBD. The capacity of new subways built in 1932-36 was largely subtracted by the removal of elevated lines, so the total rail delivery capacity into the CBD has increased only slightly since 1924.) Both the present congestion and the slow speeds of hub-bound travel during rush hours require no elaboration.

There is now general agreement among the agencies concerned that further expansion of motor vehicle capacity into the CBD is self-defeating. (For an argument of the case see **Transportation and the Manhattan Central Business District, A Regional Plan Association Policy Statement,** Regional Plan News 82, February 1966.) By contrast, the current Metropolitan Transportation Authority program will expand subway capacity from 40 to 44 tracks and suburban rail capacity from 10 to 12 tracks, the first improvements of this kind in four and six decades, respectively. This will relieve overcrowding on the most congested lines and provide some

capacity for growth. Moreover, new branch lines on the subways and higher speeds on some subway lines and most suburban rail lines will expand the tributary area of the CBD.

While adequate for the near future, this program will have to be augmented if the longer-range projections anticipated in this report are to be satisfied. For the next cycle of transit construction, technologically-radical new underground tubes operated by gravity-pneumatic propulsion are indicated in this report. By breaking the limits on acceleration and power consumption (under which any horizontal system must labor) and achieving, with conventional city station spacing, average speeds two to three times faster than present subways, such a system not only will reduce long journeys to work significantly but also will revitalize extensive "gray areas" of the Region that are now bypassed for almost equally accessible suburbs. (For a description of the gravity-pneumatic system, see L. K. Edwards, Urban Gravity-Vacuum Transit, **Transportation Engineering Journal,** American Society of Civil Engineers, No. 1, February 1969.)

As to the transportation capacity for circulation within the CBD, the potentially high concentration of office buildings suggests largely point-to-point delivery for any new system. For example, the projected 100 million square feet of additional office space if compactly located, could all be within a three-minute walk of only 10 transit stations.

With our present, haphazard development patterns that do not consciously relate private construction to public transportation, the tremendous potential for proximity which high density offers has not been fully realized. To correct that condition and to provide easy interchange between the various transit lines as well as to and from major terminals, mechanically-aided pedestrian distribution systems, like the one proposed by the City along 48th Street, are recommended. These may take the form of discrete vehicles or continuously moving accelerating belts, depending on technical considerations. Research and development work on these subsidiary systems, just as on gravity-vacuum tubes for high-speed trunkline access, deserves highest priority.

Dim Future without Design

Disjointed, single-purpose planning in the past, the failure to consciously shape the central business district as a functional and visual entity, is undermining the future of the CBD in three closely related ways:

1. Internal circulation, the very reason for a close concentration of activities, is slow, inconvenient, crowded and chaotic. Some 830,000 people enter the CBD each workday between 8 and 9 a.m., 82 percent of them underground, by subway or rail. They lose a disproportionate amount of time and encounter an overpowering amount of frustration along the journey from the train door to the elevator door. Below the surface, they are crowded into dirty, smelly, dreary mazes. On the surface, they compete with taxis, trucks, buses, handcarts and private autos. The private, air-conditioned splendor of new office lobbies contrasts starkly with the squalor of the public environment below ground and at street level.

2. The visual form of the CBD, once characterized by the clustered peaks which signify Manhattan to the world, is gradually losing its distinctiveness and giving way to "slab city"—interminable rows of identical reflecting surfaces lined up along identical blocks, all thirty to fifty stories high. It is hard to sense one's location by means other than street signs, and new public spaces, comparable to Bryant Park, Grand Central Concourse, or Rockefeller Center, are not being created. The 1961 New York City zoning resolution dispensed with the traditional "ziggurat" building shapes which had been most profitable to construct under the previous ordinance and encouraged instead setbacks at the street level. But these plazas crop up haphazardly with no relation to a consciously designed progression of spaces and with no relation to the magnitudes of pedestrian movement in each place. Low buildings, over the tops of which tall ones can be seen and "read," are rapidly disappearing. Many were architectural or historical landmarks.

The ancillary activities which the low buildings typically housed and which give flavor to the CBD — the restaurants, the bars, the specialty stores, the clubs, the studios and the theatres — often disappear along with the buildings. The 1967 zoning amendment encouraging the replacement of theatres displaced by office buildings in the theatre district, is one of the few efforts so far to stem the full effects of "slab city."

3. The pedestrian, for whom the central business district was, after all, created (even the motorist becomes a pedestrian after he parks his car) has been the forgotten man.

Underground, he is denied sunlight, fresh air, orientation, and elementary amenity. The underground world is totally isolated from the world above ground, and the narrow rat-holes of subway stairways are designed to disturb the street surface as little as possible.

Above ground, the pedestrian is denied separation from motor vehicles, protection from the elements, and a sense of place. He is deprived of chances to sit, to stroll leisurely, to relax, to look at the buildings surrounding him.

Places of interest to him at the sidewalk level, the store windows and restaurants, are increasingly giving way to marble lobbies, glassed-in banks, impersonal showrooms. He is denied the right to walk in dignity.

No provision is made for places where trees could grow with their roots in the ground or snow could stay for a few days to remind the pedestrian of seasons, indeed of any thing other than concrete and glass.

Access to the magnificent waterfronts along the Hudson and East Rivers is largely denied, even though the economic justification for that is long past.

These are among the problems to which this study is addressed.

Urban Design Principles and Prototypes

The notion of the Access Tree is the response to these problems. It embodies a set of interrelated principles of functional and visual organization. These are, briefly:

1. The tallest buildings are consciously clustered around the point of highest accessibility, such as the intersection of two transit lines. Buildings further away are kept contrastingly low. This arrangement
a. minimizes the walking distance from train door to elevator door.
b. lets the tall buildings be seen and gives them a view.
c. gives the city form clarity and an expressive image.

2. The local open spaces to which each tall building is entitled are pooled in one place, in the middle, at the point of transit access, where the pedestrian volumes are highest. This principle
a. relates pedestrian space directly to pedestrian density.
b. creates a large, useful, visual, and memorable public square, a "sense of place."

3. The public square, which the cluster of tall buildings has in common, is located **below street level,** right where the bulk of the pedestrians emerge from the underground trains. This fundamental requirement

a. provides for consistent grade-separation between pedestrians (most of whom are delivered by underground modes) and motor vehicles on surface streets.

b. brings building entrances and elevator lobbies directly to underground for the emerging rail rider.

c. breaks through the street membrane and integrates the space below ground with the space above ground to express and use the three-dimensional nature of the city center. Thus,

• pedestrians below street level are given sunlight and air,

• the shaft of light descending below ground provides orientation and identity, which do not exist now in the endless turning corridors,

• protection is afforded from inclement weather along the edges of the open wells and in connecting passages,

• the interest of the cityscape is enhanced for pedestrians at street level since they can look down as well as up, seeing a world that is now judiciously concealed,

• additional building frontage is created for retail and eating establishments now increasingly squeezed out at the sidewalk level.

The key to all these objectives is an open public square below street level and a design philosophy and institutional framework which considers the horizontal transportation by train, the vertical transportation by elevator, and their pedestrian link as parts of a single system. More broadly, this approach suggests that the entire urban infrastructure, not just the public transportation system but the water and waste, the energy and communication systems, should be viewed and designed as one "mega-building," to which the interchangeable above-ground portions of the urban structure are continuously attached, removed and again attached. Thus, the concern of urban design is less with the shapes and surfaces of individual buildings than with the form-determining, functional "guts" of the city.

Urban design amenity should be provided in other ways, too:

1. More access to nature, with

a. continuous pedestrian access to the waterfront and waterfront parks extended into the CBD.

b. spaces where trees can grow and fountains play.

c. outdoor sitting and eating spaces.

2. More protection from nature in inclement weather,

which might include

a. arcades, overhangs, covered pedestrian passages.

b. heated sidewalks in winter and air-conditioned portions of transit stations and pedestrian passageways in summer.

3. Cleaner articulation of surface movement, with

a. more pedestrian space at the sidewalk level, including mid-block pedestrian walkways.

b. creation of vehicle-free pedestrian enclaves: streets or sections of streets (e.g., those leading to major subway stations) closed to vehicular traffic, which is diverted around them or through underground expressways.

c. more differentiation of street traffic (e.g., distinguishing through streets from local service streets) with stringent controls on garage location to curtail pedestrian-garage conflicts and prevent the attraction of more vehicular traffic than the street space can handle.

d. provision of collective truck loading docks in blocks now deficient in off-street truck loading space, with a separate intra-block circulation system for goods delivery.

In addition to all these, the smaller scale concerns of conventional urban design should not be overlooked, such as signs and street furniture, a satisfying sequence of urban spaces — with appropriate rhythms of narrow and wide opening desirable views and closing undesirable ones and with ample ceiling heights in enclosed public spaces.

None of these principles is entirely new. For example, the Access Tree (minus the openness to light and air) is embodied in Grand Central Terminal, built in 1913, and also partly in Rockefeller Center, (minus transit access and the opening of underground corridors to the underground plaza). Other pertinent ideas of early architectural theorists, such as Sant' Elia, Le Corbusier and Eugene Hénard, are presented in the report, as well as related urban design developments in other cities.

Application of Principles

The design principles of this report are applied, by way of illustration, to Midtown Manhattan. Its existing physical form is first inventoried in terms of building bulk and coverage, major land uses, public rights-of-way on the surface and underground transit access, including the pedestrian areas of stations and the passenger volumes they handle. The area presently zoned for office use is then viewed with regard to the prospective permanence of existing buildings ("hard" vs. "soft" parcels), transit access and ease of land assembly. Theoretically, enough land is zoned for high office buildings to accommodate the equivalent of 66 additional Time-Life buildings projected for Midtown over the next thirty-five years. This, however, may not be realistic, given present real estate practices, nor is it advisable, given criteria of transit access and the objective of preserving desirable "low" areas. A conceptual diagram based on this reasoning suggests the reinforcement of existing office clusters near Grand Central, Rockefeller Center and Penn Station, the creation of new clusters toward the south and the west, preserving "low" areas in-between. Residential areas would be fostered in the four corners of Midtown, and parks would be developed along the waterfronts.

While it is not the object of this report to propose a transportation plan for Midtown, diagrammatic studies are presented showing the need to stage planning with a view toward an eventual unified system (not piece meal, as at present), to seek strong geometric clarity (generally lacking now), and a direct and obvious relationship of what happens below ground to what happens above ground. The coming decades will require a far-reaching reconstruction of the transportation infra-structure in Midtown, and a number of possible new facilities are suggested by way of illustration. The kind of physical form such a movement system could "grow" is indicated in a "form response diagram."

Case studies of 42nd Street and a proposed new office cluster near the Hudson River, where a large Access Tree can be built from scratch, detail the principle of integrating vertical and horizontal movements and above-ground and below-ground spaces.

Case studies at a still finer grain show how the street membrane can be cut open, the underground given light and air, and distinctive "urban rooms" or pedestrian spaces created on Lexington Avenue near 51st to 53rd Streets, between Bryant Park and Sixth Avenue, at Times Square, and at Eighth Avenue and 42nd Street.

Finally, the importance of preserving historic landmarks amidst the rapidly changing technological environment of Manhattan is emphasized and some methods cited.

Implementation

Experience suggests that distinctive building groups related to public spaces and public transportation in accordance with the principles outlined will only be built if there is a positive public policy to nurture them.

Among the obstacles are the difficulties of large-scale land assembly, secretive decision-making, the institutional walls among public agencies and between these agencies and private business (walls that end up in the form of concrete) the tendency for action to out-run design, and an incidence of costs and benefits that does not necessarily encourage the most productive capital investment for the public as a whole. A greater public role in private building operations is necessary without destroying the incentives of profit. And public agencies must work more effectively together and with private builders toward design goals.

Six specific steps are recommended:

1. Planning at the city level should be brought closer to the ground. A set of detailed business district plans are needed to guide zoning and specific developments. A permanent urban design staff is needed to conceive and negotiate opportunities along the lines of these plans. The small urban design staff New York City recently established in its Department of City Planning, following recommendations of the Paley Commission, is a successful beginning.

2. A Development Coordinator should be appointed for each business district (considering Midtown one district, Downtown another, Downtown Brooklyn and Jamaica a third and fourth). They should be responsible for coordinating the decisions of the mayor, the governor, public authorities and private enterprise.

3. Organized citizen participation is essential for each business district.

4. Incentive zoning, already used for theatres and plazas, should be developed to reward private developers with added income from their property if they attain publicly beneficial urban design objectives. The magnitude of these rewards should be scaled to the public benefit provided.

5. An official map of underground pedestrian plazas and passages should be prepared; it should have legal authority comparable to the official map of streets.

6. Taxation should not discourage good design.

An unrivalled reservoir of design talent is available in New York; what is needed is a practical way of harnessing this talent with the force of private investment to achieve a truly magnificent urban environment.

The New York Region and, to an extent not generally recognized, the entire nation, have a large stake in a vital attractive Manhattan central business district. Application of the emerging discipline of urban design is essential to realize the CBD's potential.

Note: Most of the drawings in this report were prepared on the basis of data and plans available in 1966-67. There has been no systematic updating.

1. PROJECTIONS

Let the city provide a chassis for private enterprise, combining the sites of private buildings to add up to new Grand Centrals and new Rockefeller Centers. The keys are traffic flow and common use of plaza space, already encouraged by zoning laws. We believe the financial advantages to owners who would take part in the creation of such places would in themselves be quite compelling, enhancing the worth of their properties. The legal strength of the city to enforce such a program is also clear, according to the sources we have consulted, but only if an overall design is evolved for an area before a new wave of commercial development engulfs it. The pace of the city indicates that the occasions for creating places are here and will continue; what we lack is plans.

The Threatened City
A report on the design of the City of New York by the Mayor's Task Force.
William S. Paley, Chairman, February, 1967

1. DIMENSIONS OF THE REGION'S CENTRAL BUSINESS DISTRICT

The heart of the New York Metropolitan Region is 8.6-square-mile area below Central Park—the Manhattan central business district (CBD). No urban center in the world approaches its intensity of activity.

Most of the activities in which the New York Region plays a major national role — such as finance, insurance, corporate headquarters, communications, foreign trade, wholesaling, apparel, printing, non-profit organizations, culture and entertainment—are the kinds which locate primarily in the center. In contrast, the nationally important activities in most other large metropolitan areas are of a sort which tend to be relatively dispersed, for example, aircraft in Los Angeles, autos in Detroit and metals and food processing in Chicago. In other words, more than in most areas, the CBD is the key to the economy of the entire New York Region.

Among the measures of the magnetism of the Manhattan CBD are (1) the high incomes of its workers (in 1960, the CBD had 26 percent of the employees of Regional Plan's 31-county Study Area, but 40 percent of the employees earning over $10,000 annually), (2) the trouble people take to get there (trips to the CBD are 50 percent longer than the average trip in the Region), and (3) its concentration of special activities (for example, the CBD contains 52 percent of the Region's jobs in office buildings, 76 percent of its legitimate theatres, 26 percent of its department store floorspace, 25 percent of its manufacturing/wholesaling employment and 14 percent of its college enrollment).

Future of the Manhattan CBD

Declining share of the Region's jobs. In 1965, Regional Plan's Study Area had a total of 7.8 million jobs. Regional Plan Association projects employment growth to 13.2 million by the year 2000, an increase of 5.4 million. Over this same period, jobs in the Manhattan central business district are projected to grow from 2.1 to 2.4 million, an increase of 300,000. Thus, 93 percent of the additional jobs in the Study Area are expected to locate outside the CBD. The CBD's share of total jobs will drop from 27 to 18 percent. Even jobs in office buildings, for which the CBD is especially attractive, are expected to grow faster elsewhere, with a decline in the the CBD share of the Study Area total from 52 percent in 1965 to 43 percent in 2000. This underscores the tremendous job growth for which the rest of the Region will have to plan, a subject of other reports of the Second Regional Plan.

Despite its small share of the Region's economic growth, an increase of 300,000 jobs in the Manhattan CBD is substantial. Why should it grow at all?

Offices and the Manhattan CBD. Indications are that the kinds of jobs which thrive in the CBD are among those which are growing the fastest. In 1965 there were 1.6 million jobs in office buildings in the entire Study Area. We expect this total to grow to 3.0 million by the year 2000. While there are technological advances, hence increased productivity, in office work, these do not appear to be slowing the employment growth in such white collar industries as publishing, television and other communications; government; finance and non-profit institutions.

Nor has new technology produced a substitute for face-to-face contacts. Continually improving communications vastly augment the exchange of information, but the occasions for decisions requiring direct human confrontation seem to be growing, not declining.

So, not only is the number of office jobs as a whole growing fast, but that type involving frequent contact among a large number of persons — the type which flourishes in Manhattan — is one of the most rapidly expanding office job categories. In contrast, standardized and repetitive office jobs have less need of a CBD location; these are more subject to automation and are projected to grow less than half as fast.

The Manhattan CBD is the worldwide symbol of office activity. Its 800,000 jobs in office buildings occupy about 200 million square feet of gross office space, or 160 million square feet of net rentable space. The pace of Manhattan office construction following World War II continues unabated; in fact, the rate is now faster than ever. From 1950 through 1959, 32 million square feet of rentable office space were constructed; between 1960 and 1969, 55 million square feet will have been added. Thus, while the earlier 1950-1959 annual rate of office construction averaged 3.2 million square feet, the 1960-1969 annual rate is at 5.5 million square feet. For the 1969-73 period, some 55 million square feet of office space are planned, an annual rate of about 10 million square feet. (It should be noted that Manhattan office construction is being built not only to accommodate additional employment but also to replace obsolete buildings and to increase space per worker.)

The need for a significant number of the New York Region's top jobs to be in its CBD was pointed out in the economic study conducted for Regional Plan Association by Harvard University's Graduate School of Public Administration.* As it indicated, a high proportion of the CBD's 2 million jobs are there because of the added strength they gain by being together. The CBD is where the advantages of agglomeration reach their peak.

Can the CBD's office jobs continue to grow? Should they? Our answer to both questions is yes. The conclusion appears reasonable that the economy of the Region and of the nation will be strengthened by growth in the CBD for those jobs which seem to belong in this unique center of corporate headquarters, information, entertainment, culture and commerce.

Total CBD employment. The 800,000 jobs now in office buildings in the CBD constitute but 40 percent of the CBD total. As the chart on the opposite page shows, there are also 600,000 jobs in factories and warehouses and 700,000 jobs in other types of places. These "other" jobs include a large number which are there only because of the offices and manufacturing — in restaurants, stores, entertainment and other services.

The chart indicates that the total number of jobs in the CBD remained nearly stable at about 2 million between 1959 and 1965. There was an increase of approximately 45,000 office jobs, but this was accompanied by an offsetting decline of 50,000 jobs in factories, lofts and warehouses, activities which are increasingly seeking more and cheaper space outside the CBD as they automate and become less labor-intensive. So, a growth in office jobs has not produced an increase in total CBD jobs. Actually, as near as can be determined, a relatively constant CBD employment total of around 2 million jobs probably has existed for the last few decades, as

*Raymond Vernon, *Metropolis 1985*, Cambridge, Harvard University Press, 1960.

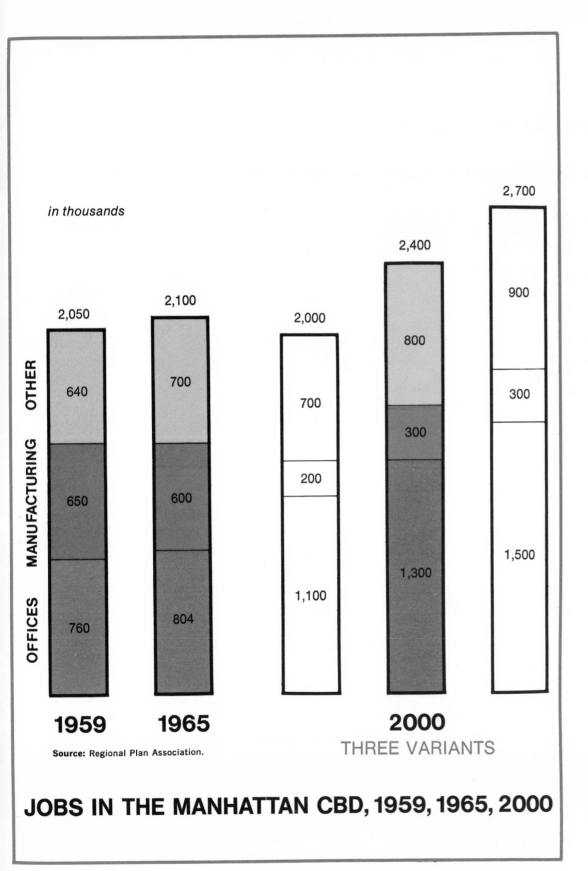

in thousands

OTHER

MANUFACTURING

OFFICES

	1959	1965	2000 (first)	2000 (second)	2000 (third)
Total	2,050	2,100	2,000	2,400	2,700
Other	640	700	700	800	900
Manufacturing	650	600	200	300	300
Offices	760	804	1,100	1,300	1,500

1959   **1965**   **2000**

THREE VARIANTS

Source: Regional Plan Association.

JOBS IN THE MANHATTAN CBD, 1959, 1965, 2000

far back as 1930.

If office jobs continue to grow at their post-World War II rate, the CBD employment total will have to increase. The number of manufacturing jobs which can be replaced by office jobs is not unlimited. Moreover, a good economic case can be made for the conclusion that CBD manufacturing will stop declining long before it reaches zero. There is a certain number of manufacturing/wholesaling jobs (we judge it to be about 200,000) which require a CBD location; these include some branches of printing and apparel as well as storage and distribution of a wide variety of goods.

With these forces in mind, Regional Plan is examining a range of growth possibilities for the CBD to the year 2000 (Chart 1). The lowest employment estimate would comprise a 300,000 increase of jobs in office buildings and a more-than-matching decline of 400,000 jobs at production sites, resulting in a decline of 100,000 in total CBD employment. At the other extreme, it is quite possible that CBD employment could reach 2.7 million, with 700,000 more office jobs. This would mean a continuation of the rate of office construction we have experienced since World War II and only a 300,000 decline in manufacturing/wholesaling jobs.

Regional Plan has chosen a middle variant for urban design purposes: a rise of 500,000 jobs in office buildings, a decline of 300,000 in manufacturing/wholesaling, an increase of 100,000 in jobs serving the added office workers, and a total employment of 2.4 million. This selected variant is based on our judgment of how many of the Region's new office jobs will need to be in its central business district. There appears to be no basis for denying the choice of a CBD location to those private, non-profit and government activities which seek the advantages of personal confrontation and the special services that are unique to Manhattan.

This economic picture of the Manhattan CBD is consistent with the reasoning and the projections of the Harvard Study.

Physical requirements of future jobs

Assuming the economic forecast to be reasonable, could it happen in physical terms? Is there enough room? Is there enough transportation capacity to the CBD? Can the area itself have efficient circulation and be attractive?

Enough room? Office space to accommodate 500,000 new office jobs not counting the replacement of old buildings and the upgrading of space standards per employee would come to about 100 million square feet of rentable office space by the year 2000, compared to the roughly 160 million square feet of rentable floor space in place in 1965 — a lot of office space, yet it would occupy relatively little of the CBD's land (see chart opposite).

Currently, office buildings occupy about .4 square miles (250 acres) or just under 5 percent of the total land area of the Manhattan central business district. The land requirements for an additional 100 million square feet of office space, based on today's typical construction and occupancy practices, would amount to less than .3 square miles (200 acres). This means that just under 9 percent of the CBD land in the year 2000 would be required for offices. Manufacturing now occupies about 1.1

square miles (700 acres), nearly three times as much land as offices. Land freed by the projected decline of 300,000 manufacturing and wholesaling jobs would, because of its much lower employment density, be more than ample for all the office growth. (Manufacturing density in the CBD averages about 900 workers per acre; new office buildings accommodate between 3,000 and 4,000 per acre.)

This is not to suggest the extent to which office construction will, or should, take place on former manufacturing sites, although the idea should be encouraged in some locations because there are many obsolescent industrial areas in Manhattan which are attractive for office activity (see Chapter 4). The attempt here is to support the conclusion that land requirements are a minor constraint on the growth of offices.

In fact, the primary concern of this report grows out of the compactness of CBD office activity. When offices are grouped in tall buildings, they increase tremendously the demands on pedestrian circulation space and pedestrian-related activities in their immediate vicinity, hence the frequent need for multi-level distribution of some activities. While the 1.5 square miles of CBD sidewalks shown in the chart on page 17 could accommodate, without crowding, far more pedestrians than even our largest CBD projection implies, this is largely an academic point. People do not use **all** of the sidewalks intensively, because the jobs are concentrated on only a small part of the CBD's land area.

The expected concentration of new office jobs also affects transportation planning; it will require that new transit capacity and solutions be estab-

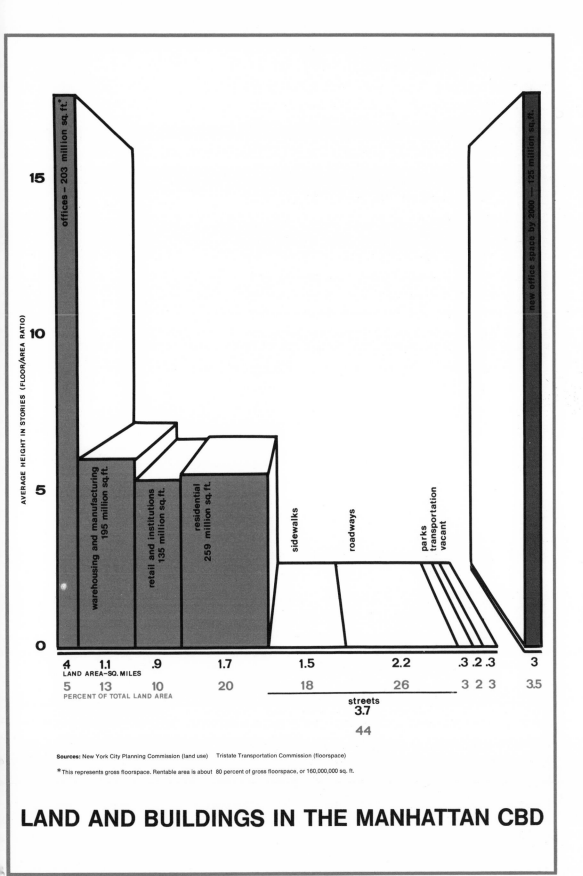

AVERAGE HEIGHT IN STORIES (FLOOR/AREA RATIO)

15

10

5

0

offices – 203 million sq. ft.*

warehousing and manufacturing 195 million sq.ft.

retail and institutions 135 million sq. ft.

residential 259 million sq. ft.

sidewalks

roadways

parks
transportation
vacant

new office space by 2000 — 125 million sq. ft.

4	1.1	.9	1.7	1.5	2.2	.3 .2 .3	3

LAND AREA—SQ. MILES

| 5 | 13 | 10 | 20 | 18 | 26 | 3 2 3 | 3.5 |

PERCENT OF TOTAL LAND AREA

streets
3.7

44

Sources: New York City Planning Commission (land use)   Tristate Transportation Commission (floorspace)

*This represents gross floorspace. Rentable area is about 80 percent of gross floorspace, or 160,000,000 sq. ft.

LAND AND BUILDINGS IN THE MANHATTAN CBD

lished at a few key points, supplemented by major new and improved secondary systems, throughout the CBD.

Enough transportation to the CBD? Probably transportation capacity has been the most important limiting factor on total employment in the Manhattan CBD. With minor exceptions, it is impossible to squeeze more workers into the trains and highways leading to the CBD — a condition too widely experienced to require elaboration.

We believe substantial transportation investment is needed to relieve overcrowding, increase speed and eliminate the ugliness of the facilities we already have and to increase the capacity to accommodate more job-destined users to and from the CBD. This report assumes the gradual conversion of the Region's rail transit and commuter railroads to modern operation and the building of several new, high-speed, technically-advanced transit systems. Detailed transportation recommendations are the subject of another volume of the Second Regional Plan.

Internal circulation and attractiveness. Assuming there is adequate land for office growth, how should it be used? Assuming more people can reach the CBD, what happens after they get there? The internal workings of the CBD — notably the circulation system — are strained now. We believe that, increasingly, the success of the Manhattan CBD will depend on people's ability to move freely and comfortably within it and to enjoy the experience of being there. To do this requires application of urban design principles to integrate activities, transportation and the city forms they produce. Such is the main purpose of this report.

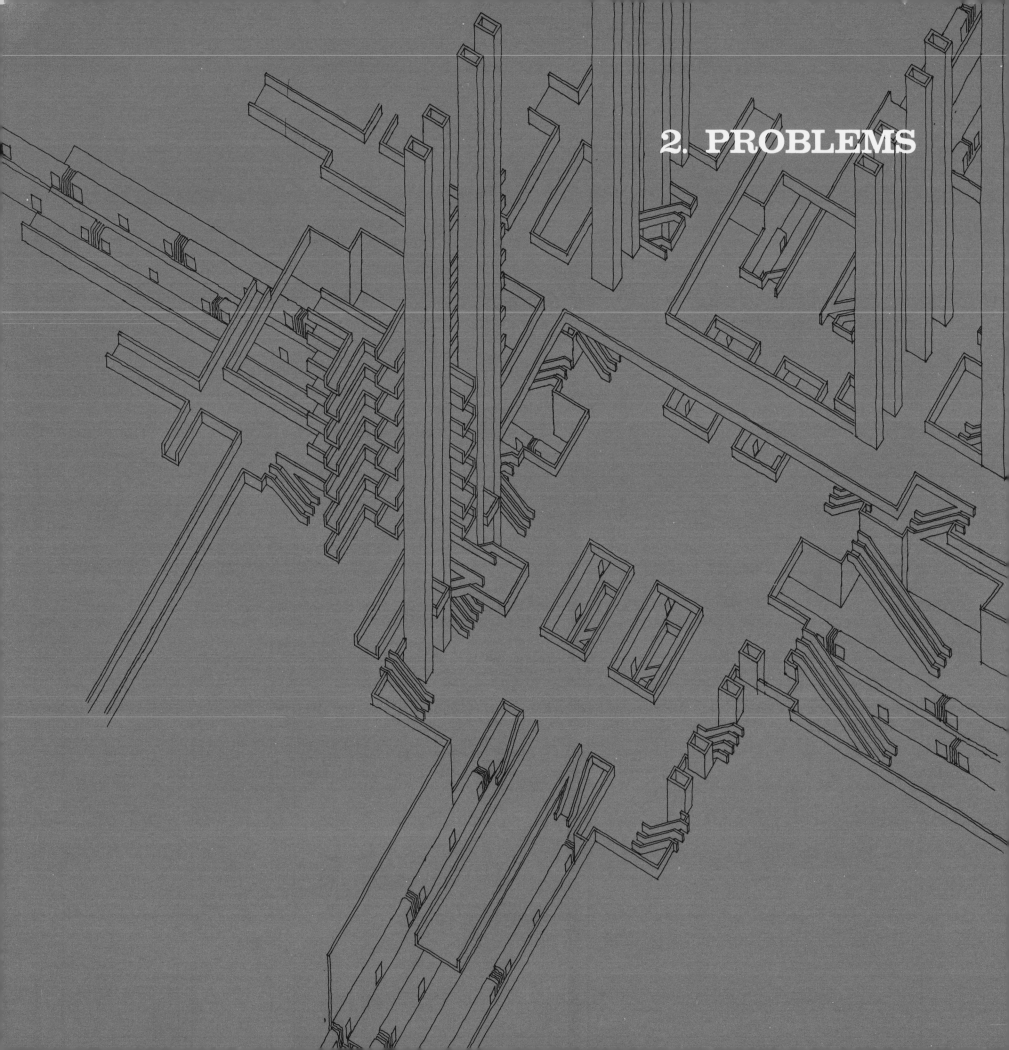

2. PROBLEMS

A DIM FUTURE WITHOUT DESIGN

The Manhattan central business district still stimulates a great deal of opportunity and excitement. But these too often occur in, and are dulled by, an inferior physical environment.

The newness and slick surfaces of contemporary building materials exaggerate the vastness of postwar office construction. On an individual basis, the new work spaces are noticeably better than the cramped, poorly lit and un-airconditioned buildings of the twenties and thirties (although few current structures equal their predecessors in over-all architectural design quality). But the main problem is not with single buildings; rather, it is with the total environment they create — a CBD of growing inconvenience, discomfort, formlessness, confusion and, often, unsafe circulation.

Failure to plan and act is undermining the CBD in three closely related ways. First, the growing malfunction of this enormous international business and pleasure machine is causing congestion and friction that increasingly stresses the limits of human tolerance. Second, the vivid imagery and distinctive form and appearance created by Manhattan's clustered office towers, which mean Manhattan in the eyes and mind of the world, are in danger of disappearing under a spreading "slab city" lacking the variety and identity of the special districts which exist today. Third, the CBD pedestrian has become the forgotten man.

Functional problems: poor circulation

The lifelines of the CBD are its channels of movement. Of the nearly 3½ million persons entering the CBD on a typical business day, 62 percent come by subway or railroad, 7 percent by bus, and 27 percent by taxi or auto. At the crucial peak hour between 8 and 9 a.m., 800,000 people enter the CBD, of whom 82 percent enter by subway or railroad. While the main part of the work trip itself to the CBD (the train, subway or bus) needs to be speeded and made more comfortable, the fact is that about half of the total travel time of the aver-

THE JOURNEY TO WORK

A disproportionate amount of time is lost as well as an overbearing amount of frustration encounted by workers *after* they arrive in the CBD. The sequence of photographs at left illustrate typical experiences on the journey to work in the Midtown area. There are some glimpses of pleasure: the monumental space of the Grand Central Concourse, the relatively spacious lobbies of new office buildings such as Pan American or Union Carbide. But on the whole, the journey is crowded, disjointed and confused. The private, airconditioned splendor contrasts sharply with the squalor of the public environment below ground and at street level. There is no effort to visually unify the public and the private domain, and to give the pedestrian a meaningful sequence of experiences.

photos by Louis B. Schlivek

age worker is taken up in getting to and from the major transportation mode, a large part of which is at the CBD end. The trip of a typical CBD worker from his train door to the station platform, through underground corridors, up the stairways to the street, along the sidewalk, into the building, up the elevator and, finally, down the hall to the office door is slow, crowded and unnecessarily stressful. The number of such trips at concentrated points within the CBD can be enormous. For example, about 80,000 people emerge from subway and railroad trains at Grand Central during the peak hour and nearly 200,000 do in the course of the typical weekday. Without adequate space or better movement machinery, the trip from the train door becomes chaotic. The toll it takes, in mind and body, ill prepares the commuter for his work or shopping venture.

The movement of taxis, private cars and other automotive vehicles is also a serious circulation problem. While only a small proportion of the people in the Manhattan CBD travel by these modes, their number is significant, and many, for business, health and other reasons, must use these modes. However, the most effective way to insure the free flow of street traffic is to divert some car users to public transportation. This can be achieved to a degree by regulation and pricing. But, in the long run, the best solution is to offer an attractive public transportation alternative. This means not only providing sufficient transportation capacity and reasonable comfort in getting people to the CBD, but ease of movement after they have arrived (at the walker's scale) — one of the subjects of this report.

Physical form problems: Slab City

Once the commuter has emerged from underground and has a chance to look around, either hurriedly on the way to work or perhaps in more leisurely fashion at lunchtime, life is not much better.

The clustered peaks which signify Manhattan to the world are gradually losing their distinct shape as they coalesce visually into an undifferentiated Midtown mass.

The new slab city pattern is epitomized on Third Avenue. Its rows of interminable reflecting surfaces have replaced the rich texture and weather-beaten variety of its former buildings; and even Park Avenue's new-era elegance becomes tedious when every building has a plaza and every lobby is transparent. The anonymous, cool surfaces of the emerging environment seem more expressive of the new machines than of the humans who control them and whose needs for human contact remain. The walker is confronted with endless surrealistic vistas of cars and more people. In very few places in the central business district can the walker sense his location by means other than street signs such as a distinct pattern of buildings and spaces. Nor are existing landmarks or transit nodes designed to create a sense of space.

PEDESTRIAN – CAR CONFLICT
(left)

Probably no problem of circulation in the Manhattan central business district is as dangerous as the daily confrontation between pedestrians and automobiles. Last year 14,846 pedestrians were injured in New York City, including 438 who were killed by cars or trucks.

The pedestrian is relegated to a very low level of importance, with traffic signals being timed for the efficient movement of cars and not people walking. Noxious exhaust fumes as well as an overbearing level of noise caused by cars, trucks and buses constantly confronts the pedestrian.

SLAB CITY
(right)

The 87 million square feet of postwar office space seems to have been scaled to and is more expressive of the computers they house than the persons who operate them. The photographs on pages 24-25 dramatize this analogy, while at the same time pointing out the architectural sterility of this unprecedented growth of office space in New York.

photos by D. H. Acheson

The gradual creep of offices threatens to produce massive single-purpose areas. As the new office structures typically limit their ground floor space to banks and an occasional expensive restaurant or showroom, the result is not only a vacuous visual environment but a dearth of choices of eating places, shops and other essential services within easy walking distance. So not only might we see the disappearance of the powerful clarity and identity of CBD clusters, such as Grand Central and Rockefeller Center, but we are faced with losing needed nearby supporting service facilities.

The plight of the relatively low height area of the theater district—threatened now by an influx of high buildings—illustrates the impending formless future. At present, it provides a vivid visual contrast to the office towers to the east by virtue of its smaller bulk and the fine-grained detail of its activities. It is also a powerful orientation element in the over-all pattern of Midtown and so helps the pedestrian know where he is. The relatively low height of buildings in the area also permits views and recognition of Rockefeller Center, the Grand Central Station-Park Avenue area and the redeveloping Penn Station office area. If the theater district is replaced by office slabs due to short-term pressures, the cost will be felt in the long run. The preservation of low areas among the high has both economic and amenity benefits for a headquarters environment.

photos by D. H. Acheson

Amenity problems: don't walk!

The needs of the man on foot have given way to those of the man behind the steering wheel. However, even car users must become pedestrians after they park. Nevertheless, sidewalks have been narrowed to accommodate motorcars, and traffic signals are timed to move automobiles, not people on foot. Where new buildings have been set back from the street, usually to gain the benefits of the more intense development of the site which zoning regulations allow, most designs inhibit easy movement into and out of the spaces; typically, walls and steps keep the pedestrian close to the stream of cars.

There are few places to escape from the crowd or to relax in an open space. Places to sit are rare. Signs one really needs are difficult to find or else undecipherable or unreadable. Major underground pedestrian corridors are crowded and have standardized low ceilings which aggravate the feeling of being trapped in the crowd. People are shut off from the remarkable waterfront which flanks the CBD. It is difficult to be visually aware of the changing seasons since there are few places to see leaves change color, for snow to remain white. Finally, the basic elements of sunlight, natural light and fresh air are unnecessarily denied the millions who must circulate both above and below ground.

These are the dis-amenities which urban design can attempt to deal with. There are, of course, other serious deficiencies which cry for attention, al-

George Tooker. The Subway. (1950.) Egg tempera on composition board. 18⅛ x 36⅛. Collection Whitney Museum of American Art, New York.

though they are not covered in this report: litter, air pollution, noise, odors and poor building maintenance, or the antiseptic total rejection of these sensory stimuli which typifies most new developments.

Conclusion

The quality of the physical environment of the Manhattan central business district affects its economic and cultural life. The more difficult and depressing the area becomes, the more it will sap the vitality and interest of its workers and other users. Manhattan's economic survival, in some form, may be assured, and if the use of the CBD is to be a dignified and pleasurable experience, good urban design is essential.

UNDERGROUND DARKNESS
(right)

Endless miles of underground pedestrian levels exist in New York which are deplorably lacking in environmental amenity. They are dark, dirty, narrow spaces which are poorly ventilated and where, at times, the overcrowding is uncivilized. The "asphalt membrane" of the street level must be penetrated to bring light and air to these heavily used underground levels.

STREET LEVEL DARKNESS
(far right)

Many pedestrian areas at street level do not receive sunlight. This basic amenity is a vital prerequisite for an active street life in our urban environment.

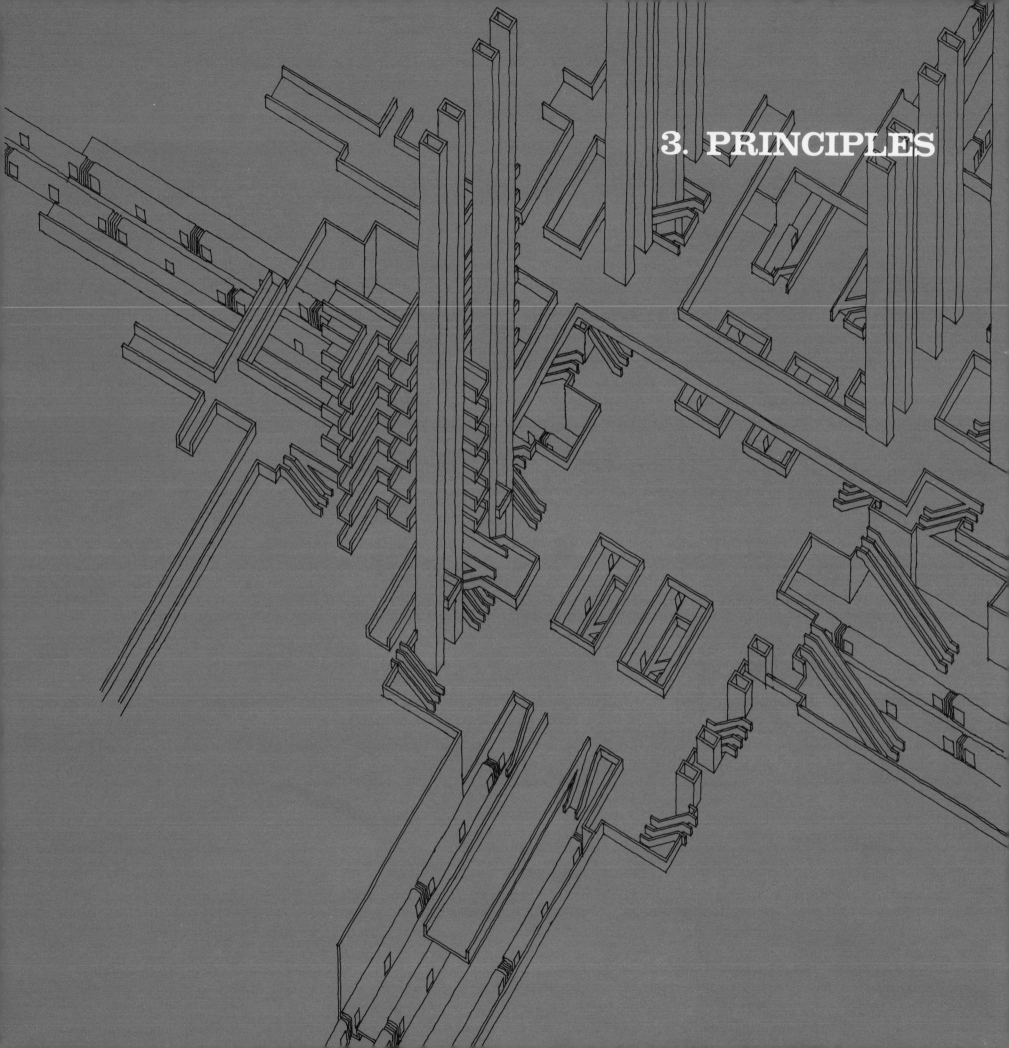

3. PRINCIPLES

URBAN DESIGN PRINCIPLES AND PROTOTYPES

This report offers three sets of design principles for the Manhattan central business district—functional, physical form and amenity. They are complementary and, of course, are not easily separable.

Functional principle: the Access Tree

The functioning of the Manhattan CBD depends on the integration of various systems of supporting facilities—its physical "infrastructure." For the most part, these systems are publicly provided (e.g., transit, streets, water and waste), although some important ones (mainly electric power and telephone) are the responsibility of private utility companies. It is a characteristic of these systems that, while they are in the public right-of-way or on other public property, they are inextricably linked to facilities on private property (an obvious example: the sewer and water lines in buildings are inseparable from those in the street). This infrastructure represents a great deal of capital, so the public has an enormous stake in the efficiency of its operation. To protect the public's investment requires not only the planning and coordination of these systems but also private development so that the whole achieves high efficiency. In this way,

the supporting facilities provided by the public can help to shape the central business district; the infrastructure is the key to the physical form of the CBD.

The primary functional system is that which makes possible the movement of people. This report pays particular attention to the circulation of workers between the train and the office. The elements of this movement path—trains, train doors, platforms, stairs, public corridors, sidewalks, building entrances, elevators and private corridors—are so closely related that they must be treated as elements of a single system in which capacity is the major design determinant. And it is a system of such size and complexity and such economic importance that it should be better understood and planned. The sensuous quality of this system is an equally important design factor, the successful manipulation of which could improve the daily lives of hundreds of thousands of daily commuters.

Several facts about the CBD underline the need for greater public planning and guidance of the train-to-office trip.

First, in areas of intense activity like the Manhattan CBD, the vast majority of workers must arrive underground. At present, 77 percent of all CBD

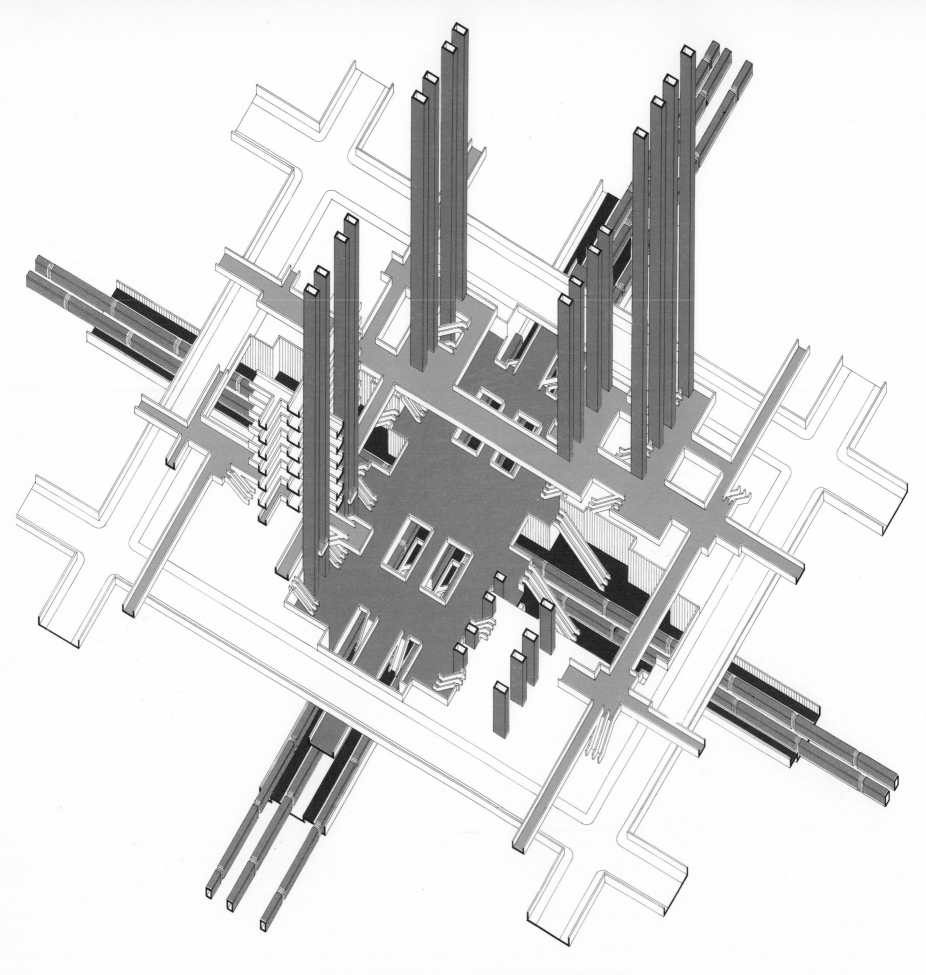

THE ACCESS TREE DIAGRAM

ACCESS TREE DIAGRAM

The circulation of workers at the peak hour between the train door and the office door, a sub-system of the total journey to work, can be compared to a tree. The analogy to the natural tree form derives from visual and morphological similarities among the several elements of each system. The natural tree's roots, trunk, branches, leaves and the fluids moving along these paths are conceptual counterparts for the underground trains and platforms, the stairs, ramps, and elevators, corridors, offices and the people who use them, of the man-made Access Tree.

The "mixing chamber" is designed to permit direct access to elevators and also to serve as the reference point for all change of modes of travel. Cutting through the street membrane and opening the "mixing chamber" to light and air would give the traveller orientation and amenity.

A major office center might have several such trees, each of which would be sized according to the capacity of its serving transit facilities, and to desired physical form. With regard to architectural form, the Access Tree would cluster large buildings tightly around the open space of the "mixing chamber," keeping more distant buildings low for the purpose of minimizing access time and achieving visual contrast.

▮ vertical movement — elevators

▮ horizontal movement — transit

▮ pedestrian mezzanine level

▮ pedestrian second level

workers use an underground train as the final mechanical transportation mode in getting to work (74 percent subway and 3 percent commuter rail). The remaining workers end their trip to the CBD as follows: 12 percent by bus, 4 percent by auto, 2 percent by ferry, 2 percent by taxi and 4 percent walk all the way.* Despite its importance to so many people, this underground world is virtually ignored in CBD planning. Current zoning policies and other planning decisions tend to be based on what happens at the street level. Planning thinking must penetrate the street membrane to the crucial transportation facilities and pedestrian circulation below ground.

Second, with the increasing dominance of office activities in the CBD, employment is growing more concentrated, hence certain subway stations and train terminals are experiencing higher pedestrian volumes than ever at peak periods. This makes planning for circulation all the more crucial.

Third, several separate trends in office building location, design and technology seem to be facilitating train-to-office planning. With greater clustering of offices, elevator stacks and station areas are inevitably closer together. The buildings are flexible in their interior arrangement through demountable partitioning and zoned environmental control, thus permitting easy adjustment of elevator location. The gross space requirements and over-all floor plans of most commercial office buildings have become relatively standard and predictable, so that loca-

---

*These figures for final mode are for workers only and are not the same as earlier ones showing mode of entry for all persons coming to the CBD, e.g., some people enter the CBD by bus but change to a subway before walking to the office.

tions of elevator shafts can often be assumed in advance of an actual building design.

The principle which responds to emerging pedestrian circulation needs and opportunities in the Manhattan central business district is the "Access Tree." The accompanying diagram shows the relation of trains and underground paths (roots), elevators (trunks) and streets or office building corridors (branches). The Access Tree is a principle for dealing with several functional problems of the CBD. In general, it is a way to plan for efficient circulation, enhanced job choice and the great social interaction which is a requirement of an office center. Also, it shows the importance of taking the underground into account; it demonstrates the relationships among the various modes of transportation within the center, proposing grade separations which favor pedestrian paths; it indicates the relationships among the various parts of the main pedestrian movement system; and it demonstrates the linkages between the essentially horizontal public transportation system and the vertical circulation in private buildings.

Other elements of the CBD infrastructure can be, and occasionally are, designed as sub-systems, including street traffic, goods movement and the flow of water, waste, power and information. If the design of the major systems were coordinated, the inherent form-determining power of the CBD's infrastructure could be consciously exploited to achieve selected urban design objectives. One such objective at the CBD scale is the idea of high clusters amid low areas.

drawing by Emil Lowenstein

INFRASTRUCTURE — MANHATTAN

UNDERGROUND
HERALD SQUARE
(right)

The analogy between the roots of trees and the man-made infrastructure becomes quite evident in this drawing by Emil Lowenstein. The tunnels and utilities can be thought of as existing roots of the Access Tree.

UNDERGROUND MIDTOWN
(left)

This dramatic cross-section through New York along 34th Street illustrates the vast and extensive public infrastructure needed to support the existing density of offices and residences for Manhattan, existing roots for future Access Trees.

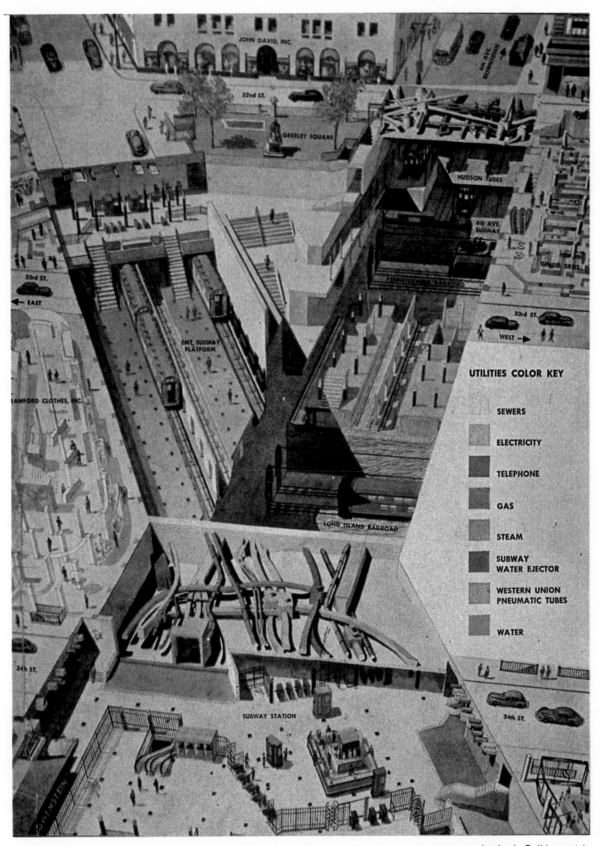

drawing by Emil Lowenstein

INFRASTRUCTURE—HERALD SQUARE

Physical form principle: Highs and Lows

The Access Tree as a functional response to the problem of office clustering provides both a framework for and a determinant of visual form principles for the CBD. The need to improve visual coherence and "grasp" of the area, to increase the sense of identity of individual parts of the CBD, to provide visual variety, to create new urban open spaces and views—all of these problems of form call for a few large clusters of office buildings and related facilities within the CBD rather than for an even spread over a large area. Our physical form principle of "highs and lows," or a few really high clusters such as Grand Central or Rockefeller Center separated by areas with low buildings and some open space, is the physical form counterpart of the functional principle which makes the tendency to cluster more efficient and workable.

As has been stated, it is very difficult to separate visual and functional considerations. The lows have an important functional as well as visual aspect. These are the places today (e.g., the Times Square theater district in Midtown and the Chambers Street area Downtown) where a wide range of essential and specialized small-scale activities locate, including eating places, theaters, small hotels and scores of different kinds of stores. A minute percentage of such activities is customarily accommodated in new office buildings, and it does not appear likely that this percentage will be increased by much in the future. Yet the office workers need these ancillary activities. If the outward creep of office buildings continues and the restaurants and stores are driven to the con-

tinually more distant edges, these facilities will be too far away for many CBD employees. If restaurants, one of the essentials of any downtown, are replaced by company cafeterias in the upper floors of office buildings, then the eating experience will become just as sterile as the visual one, and the likelihood of doing other things in the lunch hour will be diminished.

Of course, where buildings in the needed low areas have fallen into disrepair, or threaten to do so, measures should be taken to assure their rehabilitation or replacement. This is not in praise of blight, but of the small and varied among the large and standard, of some old amid the new.

Amenity principle: the pedestrian, the forgotten man

Amenity is used here to denote urban design elements which transcend strictly utilitarian considerations. The objective is to facilitate the relations between people in the central business district and their fellows as well as with the natural and built environment in ways that will be characterized by dignity, grace and a minimum of stress.

An improved relationship with nature calls for minimizing visual and physical barriers between man and the sun, sky, trees, grass and water. Underground areas should be brightened, not just with more artificial light but by the sun and sky. There should be adequate parks and the Hudson and East Rivers should be made more easily accessible.

Access to nature will be easiest to provide in good weather. However, there should be better protection against inclement weather. The Access

ROCKEFELLER CENTER

This early photograph demonstrates the clarity of physical form inherent in clustering office space. The retention of "low" service facilities in close proximity to the "high" commercial office center has not been followed in the later additions to this complex along Sixth Avenue.

35

Tree could be a totally controlled environmental envelope, and as one moved away from the core systems, more exposure would be possible. Totally exposed areas (major parks, the waterfront) might have controlled spaces within them. The effort should be to provide detailed urban design elements which will permit a range of protection against bad weather conditions while allowing positive access to nature when the conditions are favorable.

Provision of weather-oriented amenities requires a subtle combination of man-made and natural elements. Trees, water and other elements can modify the effects of wind, sun and driven rain or snow. Arcades, overhangs, walls and covered passages can offer protection from precipitation and severe temperatures. Fountains can provide a sense of heat relief and their spray may actually cool the passerby. Wide circulation paths can lower human density and reduce the effect of body heat. Rest areas can facilitate recovery from heat-induced fatigue. Radiant-heated sidewalks can eliminate ice hazards and make winter walking more pleasant.

Visual amenities can be divided into essentially utilitarian items and those which are primarily aesthetic. Signs, symbols, patterns, textures or three dimensional arrangements which have to do with important public information regarding safety or orientation should take precedence in their size, placement, frequency and inherent design characteristics.

The senses of hearing and smell should also be taken into account in CBD design. Desired sounds and odors,

such as those of nature or good food, should be accommodated; undesirable ones, such as noxious motor vehicle fumes, industrial odors and the noise of machines, should be discouraged.

Space and its distribution are crucial amenities. Beyond the functional requirement of providing the largest surface area at points of highest walking densities, and of doing so at generous standards, there is also the question of the vertical dimension — ceiling height. As a general rule, in order to prevent the possible psychological strain from crowding under low ceilings, standardized heights in spaces accommodating large assemblages of people should be avoided. Opportunity to experience relatively vast spaciousness should also be provided, for example, at the riverfronts.

Finally, there is the need to relax, to sit. Many more opportunities to pause can be designed into the CBD environment, not just in parks but on sidewalks and in other public places.

CENTRAL PARK

The most important amenity in Manhattan is Central Park, at least until the riverfronts have been reclaimed for public use. This oasis of green, which forms the northern boundary of the central business district, makes living and working in Manhattan bearable for many New Yorkers. Grand Army Plaza at the southeastern tip of Central Park is shown above.

PALEY PARK
(right)

A reaffirmation of belief in the city and the fact that it can be a much more human place to live and work is shown by this small vest pocket park on 53rd Street. Micro-amenities, because of their immediate possibilities for implementation, can become vital components in restructuring New York.

photo by Louis B. Schlivek

37

Antecedents and prototypes

Elements of the principles in this report are present in the work of several theorists and planners and in actual developments.

Second Regional Plan. Like the concepts in this report on the Manhattan CBD, Regional Plan Association's proposals in its Second Regional Plan for the entire New York Metropolitan Region are based on the idea of functional and visual clustering of major activities. "Highs" would be surrounded by low residential development and open space. Under the Plan, there would be a network of some twenty-five large, suitably spaced centers linked to regional transportation facilities — in effect, small-scale applications of the Access Tree principle. The beginnings of such a network already exist in the Region.

At the scale of the Boston-to-Washington Atlantic Urban Region, the Association also foresees that the present clustering of metropolitan areas will continue. The individual metropolises will not merge but will retain their identities, and their central business districts will remain preeminent, economically, culturally and visually.

Grand Central. The Grand Central Terminal complex, built between 1903 and 1913, is the conceptual archetype of integrated multi-level development, mixed activities and direct mass transportation access. It has yet to be surpassed either in its original or its present form, although its success is beginning to overrun it as many of its elements have become overcrowded with people and signs in recent years.

The flow of train passengers of unprecedented volume was carefully designed so that people could move with ease, and often in an atmosphere of grace and grandeur. The basic elements of the Access Tree principle can be seen in the high capacity sub-surface transportation lines, the vast mixing chamber of the great concourse where pedestrians can move in random directions and the escalator to elevator banks of the Pan Am building or underground passage connections to nearby buildings. All that is missing is more conscious architectural organization of the buildings above, as in the early Rockefeller Center. In addition to the attention paid to the multi-level pedestrian paths, the Grand Central concept incorporated a very wide range of activities both in and around the terminal, including the initiation for this purpose of the use of sixty acres of air rights (formerly, the wide trackage leading into the terminal was exposed and traversed by catwalks). The original plan anticipated today's office buildings, hotels, restaurants, banks, shops and multitudinous services. Twenty-one buildings are tied directly to the main concourse today.

William J. Wilgus, New York Central's chief engineer at the turn of the century, had the vision to see the potential of this site and promulgated many of the specific concepts. He wrote the program for a design competition which was won by Reed and Stem, who later associated with the firm of Warren and Wetmore in the actual design.

CLUSTERING AT THE REGIONAL SCALE

The principle of functional and visual clustering of major activities is consistent at all scales with the natural locational tendencies of urban development. This regional model of non-residential floor space illustrates the clustering tendency. It was constructed by the Tri-State Transportation Commission from the data of its 1963 floor space inventory. The model shows how much floor space in non-residential buildings is contained in each square mile in the Region. The model extends from New Brunswick, at the lower left, to Bridgeport and New Haven at the upper right. The two peaks in Manhattan (Downtown and Midtown) are clearly visible in the center.

39

drawing by Emil Lowenstein

drawing by Ray Pioch

A PROTOTYPE ACCESS TREE: GRAND CENTRAL STATION

The rendering above shows the double-level loop system of tracks as well as how each movement system is meshed into Grand Central on different levels.

The perspective section below shows the "mixing chamber" or grand concourse level and how this reference level extends out to integrate other buildings in the complex.

The schematic plan at the right shows the horizontal movement systems: regional trains, metropolitan subways and local shuttles are indicated in blue. The grand concourse level (reference plenum) and its extension to 21 buildings in the complex are shown in gold, with the vertical movement system (elevators) in red. The image conveyed by this diagram is one of a single organism, or more simply, one building. This preoccupation with organic integration of all the various movement systems has made Grand Central the prototype of all multi-level, multi-use urban distribution centers.

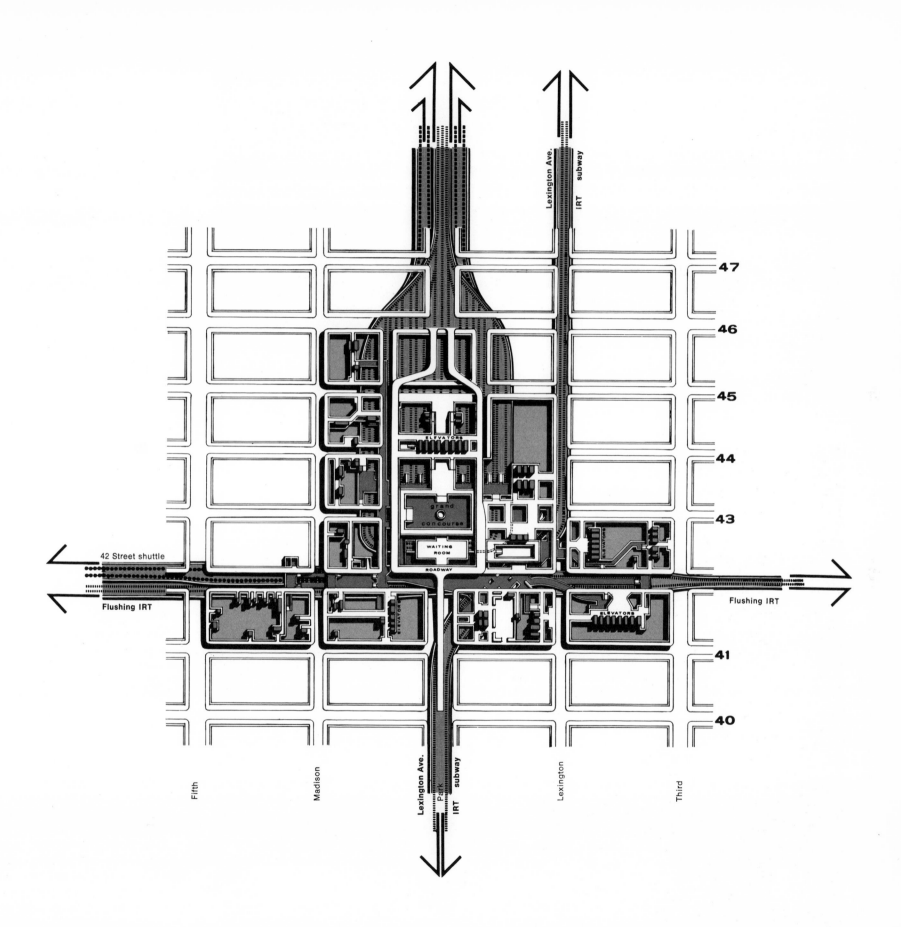

47

46

45

44

43

42 Street shuttle

Flushing IRT

ELEVATORS

grand concourse

WAITING ROOM

ROADWAY

ELEVATORS

ELEVATORS

ELEVATORS

Flushing IRT

41

40

Lexington Ave.   IRT   subway

Fifth

Madison

Lexington Ave.   Park   IRT   subway

Lexington

Third

GRAND CENTRAL VERTICAL AND HORIZONTAL MOVEMENT SYSTEMS   41

Grand Central was built in a period of our history when the private sector made many decisions now made by public agencies. Even though government, at all levels, was involved in the decisions to build the railroad and the terminal, these transportation and development decisions were the products of the imagination of private business. Now this is no longer possible. Urban transportation has shifted to where the main decisions are a public responsibility and the public's role in development is also increasing. Government is challenged to provide the vision and the leadership demanded by its new responsibilities.

First Regional Plan. The design volume of the first **Regional Plan of New York and Its Environs**, published in 1931, showed a major concern for many of the principles put forward in this volume. The need for vertical separation of the different forms of transportation was clearly enunciated. There were many proposals to ease the life of the pedestrian in the Manhattan central business district, including the creation of a separate, upper level pedestrian system in areas of most intense pedestrian traffic; arcading of buildings and other architectural solutions; the introduction of open spaces and other amenities; the opening of underground areas to light and air.

Theorists: Sant' Elia, LeCorbusier, Hénard. Several early architect innovators were able to anticipate the complex urban world to come and proposed seminal concepts for its design and organization.

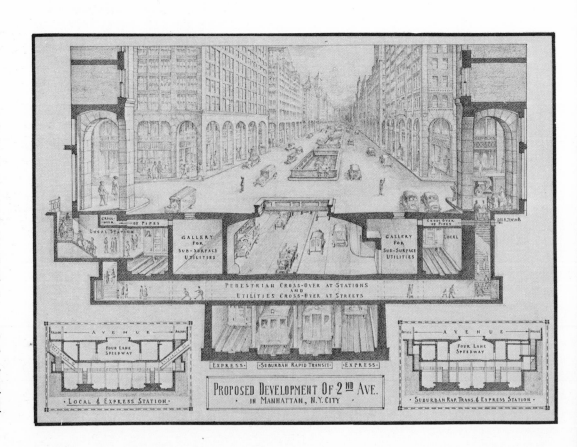

FIRST REGIONAL PLAN
(top left)

To reduce the friction among pedestrians and cars, trucks and buses, a second level walkway was proposed for the Times Square district in 1929. Though one would not necessarily endorse its design, the principle of giving the pedestrian light and air as well as safe movement throughout such dense parts of the city is as relevant today as when this proposal was published.

FIRST REGIONAL PLAN
(bottom left)

This first Regional Plan proposal for Second Avenue would have integrated new local and long-distance public transit with automobiles, pedestrianways and utilities. The elaborate arcading at street level shown in this perspective-section would have provided needed protection from the inclement weather in New York. The openings in the middle of the Avenue would have opened the underground world to sunlight.

SANT' ELIA
(right)

Clear articulation and expression of the horizontal and vertical movement systems places Sant' Elia's work foremost in the development of principles set forth in this publication.

The work of Antonio Sant' Elia, the Italian Futurist, emphasized, in 1914, the need for movement, mobility and change in the planning of city centers. Reyner Banham has noted that "far from trying to inhibit movement, Sant' Elia is basing his whole design on a recognition of the fact that in the mechanized city **one must circulate or perish.** He seems to have foreseen the technological cities of the fifties...."[*] Elsewhere, Sant' Elia's ideas have been characterized as "Grand Central with the Beaux Arts wraps taken away."

The Swiss-French architect, LeCorbusier, strongly advocated a separation of movement modes based on relative speed.[**] However, in his emphasis on park-like settings for skyscrapers and near-glorification of the motor car, LeCorbusier was reacting negatively to the substandard quality of transit. He saw the automobile as a means of achieving individuality and mobility but, as indicated earlier, its low capacity requires that it play only a subsidiary role in the largest, densest urban centers.

Eugene Hénard, who was the city architect of Paris just before World War I, also foresaw some of the implications of new forms of transportation (including the helicopter) and proposed designs which separated modes of transport and related them to dense urban activity.

Contemporary developments. There are several recent designs that reflect principles advocated here, and some are illustrated in adjacent pages.

Rockefeller Center (whose construction was begun in 1931 and is still being expanded) is notable, in our context, for its use of the level below grade to link all nineteen buildings of the complex, with their 10 million square feet of floor space, by a pedestrian concourse which is lined with shops and restaurants.

More recent projects include the Barbican scheme in London, which was built by the London County Council in the early 1960's. The Barbican involves several office and apartment towers whose pedestrian level, including plazas and shops, is raised above the street.

In Philadelphia, the Penn Center office development is designed to bring activity and natural light into the underground train level. In the same city, the proposed Market East redevelopment uses essentially the same principles as those recommended in this report.

Seattle is also considering the Access Tree and related ideas in planning CBD stations in its new transit system.

The new Montreal subway reaches a new peak in ennobling the underground passenger life in its generous use of space, high-level illumination, attractive surfaces, good graphics and generally high architectural quality. Montreal's Place Ville Marie develops the principle of integrated circulation between transit and office elevators to high standards of visual design and functional efficiency.

In Oakland, California, the City Center Project proposes to integrate vertical office and hotel circulation with transit station and freeway access underground.

[*]Reyner Banham, *Architectural Review*, May 1955.
[**]LeCorbusier, *La ville radieuse*, 1922.

HENARD

A humanist, Hénard saw movement in the city as a total energy system. A concern with safe movement of people is foremost in his theoretical work, yet at the same time he systematically studied collection and redistribution of waste materials in the city. He had an advanced understanding of small aircraft as extensions of vertical movement.

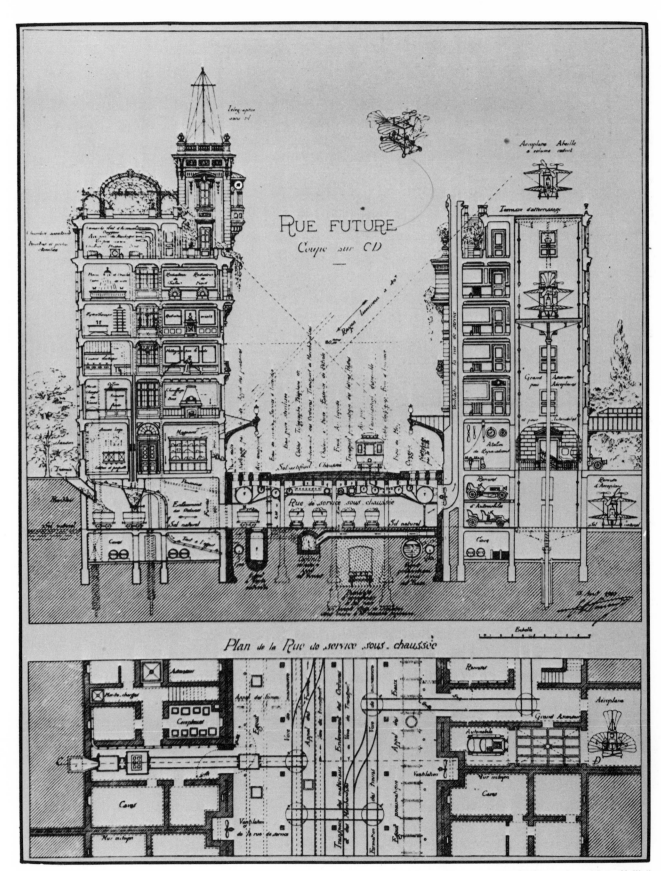

reproduction courtesy of Peter M. Wolf

MONTREAL
(left)

Probably the best contemporary example of great amenity in a rapid transit system is in Montreal. Tall ceilings in the stations provide a spacious feeling. Although the street membrane is not cut open because of the severe winters, underground levels are inter-connected by openings, as in this view, to provide orientation. Land above the stations is reserved in public ownership for future lease to private developers, who would be required to connect their lobbies and elevator banks with the infrastructure of the public subway spaces.

OAKLAND CITY CENTER
(right)

The "form determinants" that generated this proposal were the confluence of the regional rapid transit system and new freeway access in the center of Oakland. The corresponding "form response" provides clear articulation and identity of the horizontal and vertical movement systems, which would, in turn, accommodate and guide unpredictable growth and change. The scale of the development was a direct response to high access potential as well as conscious design policy to reinforce districts of high density. The collection and redistribution of persons throughout the complex is handled one level above grade.

A series of urban design studies on east Market Street in Philadelphia have explored multi-level circulation and the impact of high accessibility from various transportation modes. This section perspective clearly delineates the relationship at various levels of pedestrian concourses, subway, commuter rail, vehicular and truck access, and vehicular storage. Direct elevator access is provided to all levels which link underground transit, shopping and office areas.

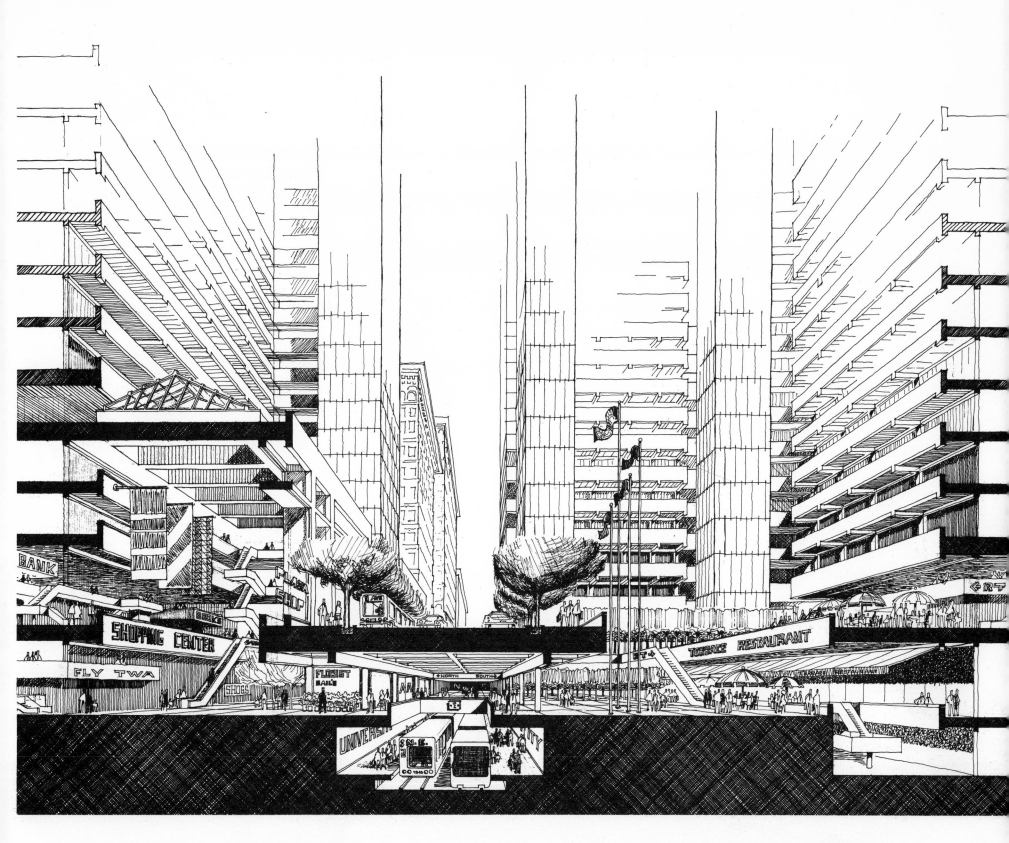

This urban design investigation of how to mesh new rapid transit into the central business district of Seattle, Washington combined the principles of urban infrastructure design and the access tree. A variety of climatized spaces were analyzed to insure pedestrian use during inclement weather.

SEATTLE CENTRAL BUSINESS DISTRICT

4. APPLICATION

THE PRINCIPLES AND THE FORM HYPOTHESIS

The design principles emphasized in the previous chapter relate to the basic recommendation of the Second Regional Plan — that major urban activities be clustered in large centers rather than dispersed. The principles also conform to general tendencies of present regional development. And they are relevant to the future functioning of the Region's economy, with the growing dominance of office work.

Physical factors

The broad, flat topography which characterizes most of the Region dramatizes the major existing activity nodes which rise as peaks from its surface. (See Tri-State model on p. 39.) Lower Manhattan, Midtown, Newark and downtown Brooklyn can be seen limed against the sky from many points throughout the Region. From an urban design point of view, the first and most striking impact of the Manhattan CBD probably is its physical appearance. Individual buildings and groups of buildings are higher and more concentrated than in any other place in the world.

Coming in closer, one can observe that there is clustering of office buildings even within Midtown. The Grand Central Station area and Rockefeller Center stand as relatively distinct and recognizable groups of office towers among their lower neighbors.

These clusters suggested the high-low principle for CBD physical organization. Even on a regional scale, large clusters can have an aesthetic impact because improved regional transportation will enable more people to actually see and know the Region's form. The principle conforms to and strengthens the dominant physical image of New York which exists in the minds of inhabitants and visitors alike. The high-low principle could offer a powerful urban design tool capable of ordering and imparting diversity and definition to a relatively flat and undifferentiated landscape. Such a juxtaposition of high and low structures in perceivable groups could provide a useful memorable image as well as an aesthetically more pleasing spectacle.

Functional factors

Just as the dominant physical characteristics of the Region suggest the design principles recommended here, so do the dominant functional factors of office employment.

Although usually unplanned, the considerable concentration of office activities in major centers of the Region and within the largest center, Manhattan's central business district, fulfills a function. Many types of office activities need to be close to related activities and to be near points of high accessibility. For such office

LOWER MANHATTAN
(left)

The highly memorable form of the clustered towers of Lower Manhattan results from the high degree of transit access on the confined site and the requirement of frequent face-to-face communications in daily financial transactions.

THE "VALLEY"
(right)

The predominantly residential and partly industrial "Valley" between Midtown and Lower Manhattan serves as a City-scale "low," giving contrast and identity to the high business clusters to its north and south. At the same time, the existing activities in the Valley functionally complement the office clusters, providing housing, printing, warehousing and wholesaling services.

photo by Louis B. Schlivek

MIDTOWN FROM THE EAST
(left)

The east side of Midtown has almost reached saturation in office space. To continue large scale office growth in this area, without improving access and internal circulation, would erode and further aggravate the functional efficiency of this area.

MIDTOWN FROM THE WEST
(right)

The west side of Manhattan, specifically the area between Eighth Avenue and the Hudson River, is not heavily built up; it contains much obsolete housing, some mixed industrial uses, and occasional vacant lots. With improved transportation, the area could exploit the unique scenic qualities of the Hudson River, now hidden behind old piers and the elevated highway.

EXISTING CLUSTERS IN MIDTOWN
(far right)

The form of clusters within clusters is revealed in Midtown, where Rockefeller Center, Penn Station and Grand Central stand out within the over-all cluster of Midtown.

photos by Louis B. Schlivek

Pennsylvania Station

Rockefeller Center

Grand Central

activities — and they are particularly those that seek out the Manhattan central business district (headquarters and other policy-making establishments) — clustering is valuable.

Factors affecting CBD form

Within the CBD, the existing form is a direct response to three added factors: accessibility, land availability and the environmental amenity of a particular area.

These three factors, in addition to the advantages to related enterprises of being close together, have resulted in clustering of office towers within Manhattan.

Accessibility in the CBD means primarily that offices have clustered around the station areas.

The phenomenon of the "Valley," a basin of low buildings between the peaks of Lower Manhattan and Midtown, illustrates a special aspect of accessibility to which the CBD's form has responded. The stations in the Valley are capable of handling many more riders, but the subway lines serving the area are at capacity during peak periods. People get off just before the trains arrive in the Valley — from Brooklyn they get off in Lower Manhattan, from the Bronx and Queens they get off in Midtown. So what lies between remains a valley between job clusters, its labor force having been intercepted at each end.

Availability of large parcels of land. The second factor that seems to have influenced office location and therefore the form of the CBD is the availability of land in large parcels. A dramatic example is the rapid development around Grand Central Terminal and up Park Avenue from the Terminal. The land was owned by a single corporation, the New York Central Railroad.

Penn Center in Philadelphia and the Penn Station area in New York are similar examples of the effect of single ownership of key large parcels on the way a central business district grows.

The influence of high accessibility and easily obtained land, assisted by fairly tight development controls, is illustrated by the apartment boom at a station on Toronto's new subway line, shown in the photographs on page 57. The photographs were taken over a period of ten years.

Amenity and image factors. The third factor determining CBD form consists of advantages beyond accessibility and land availability that one part of the CBD might have over another. These include both physical amenities (e.g., a park, a river, good shops and restaurants nearby) and abstract advantages, the "image" of an area. For example, the big office boom moved east from Grand Central Terminal, though there is more transportation capacity west of Fifth Avenue, primarily for image reasons. The expansion of central business districts in the direction of high-income residential areas is a familiar phenomenon in American cities. Now that a flurry of building has begun on Sixth Avenue, the office boom is mainly moving down from Rockefeller Center, an anchor of respectability and imageability. An address in the Wall Street area provides a clear image; a Grand Central area address provides a different but equally strong image. These images, abstract though they are, do influence development patterns. A good image is objectively observable when rents or land values are higher in one place than for comparable space in another part of the CBD; there are a number of places where this is true.

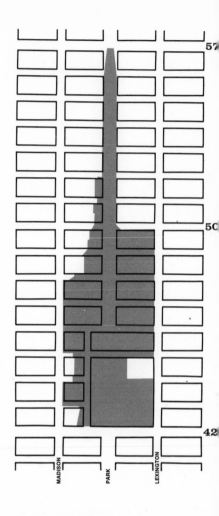

LAND OWNERSHIP AS LOCATION INFLUENCE

On much of this land, owned by the Penn-Central Railroad, postwar office development has taken place. Development is encouraged and usually speeded when a single owner is in control of a large enough tract of land to build an office tower.

CLUSTERING AROUND TRANSIT ACCESS
(right)
A very clear example of clustering at points of high accessibility is in Toronto at the Davisville Station of the recently built Yonge Street subway line. Both improved access and available land stimulated the apartment boom shown in these photographs.

Non-office activities

So far, the analysis has dealt mainly with office buildings. The way other CBD activities fit into the whole follows their function, too. For example, Fifth Avenue, the major shopping street, is relatively low amid the sky-scrapers. This allows more sunlight to fall on window-shoppers. The theater district also is low. Restaurants of all price ranges and specialty shops pro-liferate in the low buildings among the tall.

The basic form at several scales

The basic form of the Region, then, is a series of clusters. The largest consist of high buildings, mainly offices, sur-rounded by somewhat lower ones — de-partment stores and apartments. Sur-rounding the large business clusters are low apartments and one-family houses, low shopping centers, factories and local offices.

The basic form of the largest of those regional clusters, Manhattan's central business district, itself is made up of two huge clusters of high office build-ings, Midtown and Lower Manhattan, surrounded by somewhat lower build-ings.

And within the larger of these two clusters, Midtown, three clusters can be seen, Grand Central, Rockefeller Center and Penn Station, with channels and basins of "lows" among them.

This form arises from functional considerations and gives rise to the strong physical sense of the Region, of the City and of the CBD. Aesthetically and functionally, the clustering is bene-ficial.

photo by Stan Shabronsky

EMPLOYMENT DENSITY
(left)

This model by Ernst Hacker, New York City Planning Commission, portrays job density in the Manhattan Central Business District. The model (60th Street, the northern boundary of the CBD, is at right) clearly shows the twin Wall Street and Midtown peaks and the "industrial valley" between.

CONCEPTUAL DIAGRAM

Reinforcement of the distinctive "highs" of the Midtown and Downtown office centers is shown diagramatically, by the present and future office clusters within these two centers. The Valley in between should remain low, retaining some of its present economic activities, mainly light manufacturing and warehousing, and increasing its housing and institutional use. Housing best fits the transportation situation of the Valley because subways going in both directions have delivered their main load of passengers by the time they arrive there, so residents would have uncrowded trains either to Midtown or to Lower Manhattan. The Fifth Avenue spine of Midtown and the Broadway spine of Lower Manhattan (light blue) are conceptualized as primarily for pedestrian enjoyment, with lower buildings providing shops, restaurants and other services. The waterfronts (light green) would be reclaimed for public recreational use.

HIGHS

    major office clusters

    secondary office clusters

LOWS

    mixed commercial activities (shops, restaurants, hotels, theaters, etc.)

    public open space

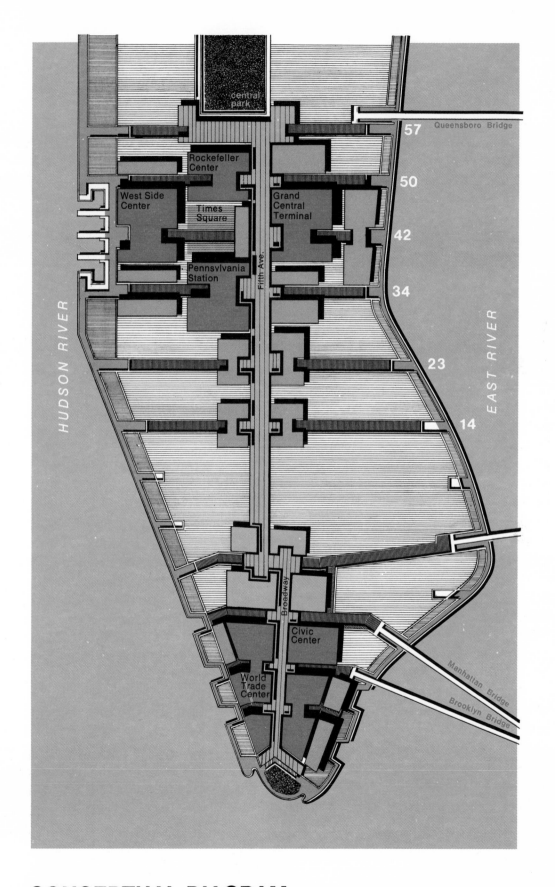

CONCEPTUAL DIAGRAM
MANHATTAN CENTRAL BUSINESS DISTRICT

MIDTOWN MANHATTAN

To demonstrate the application of the functional, physical form and amenity principles set forth in this volume, several scales were chosen. The first and largest scale of application was Midtown Manhattan. Midtown Manhattan was subjected to much more careful study than the whole of the CBD because Lower Manhattan already has a plan, prepared for and accepted by the City Planning Commission, and because the Valley does not seem an appropriate place for the dramatic increase in office jobs to be accommodated in the coming decades.

The conception at the Midtown scale—not to be considered a plan but an illustration of the principles—involved relating the distribution of activities to the existing and future circulation systems.

The urban design methodology used was first to inventory the existing physical form characteristics, followed by an analysis of the functional areas and the existing movement systems characteristics. After studying the variables of the economic projections, the commercial zoning envelope was tested to see if present zoning could incorporate the future growth.

A synthesis of this information became the conceptual diagram, whose basic underlying principles as well as physical form implications were the guidelines for structuring the future movement systems. Finding a strategy to guide the form over time towards the conceptual diagram finally produced the diagramic form response. This is a much finer grain look at the future physical form, yet again it must be qualified as a diagram, not a plan.

EXISTING PHYSICAL FORM
(right)

Grand Central, Rockefeller Center, and Pennsylvania Station emerge as distinct clusters in midtown today.

Underlying these existing clusters are elaborate regional and metropolitan movement systems. These special destinations in midtown provide a wide choice of modal interchange.

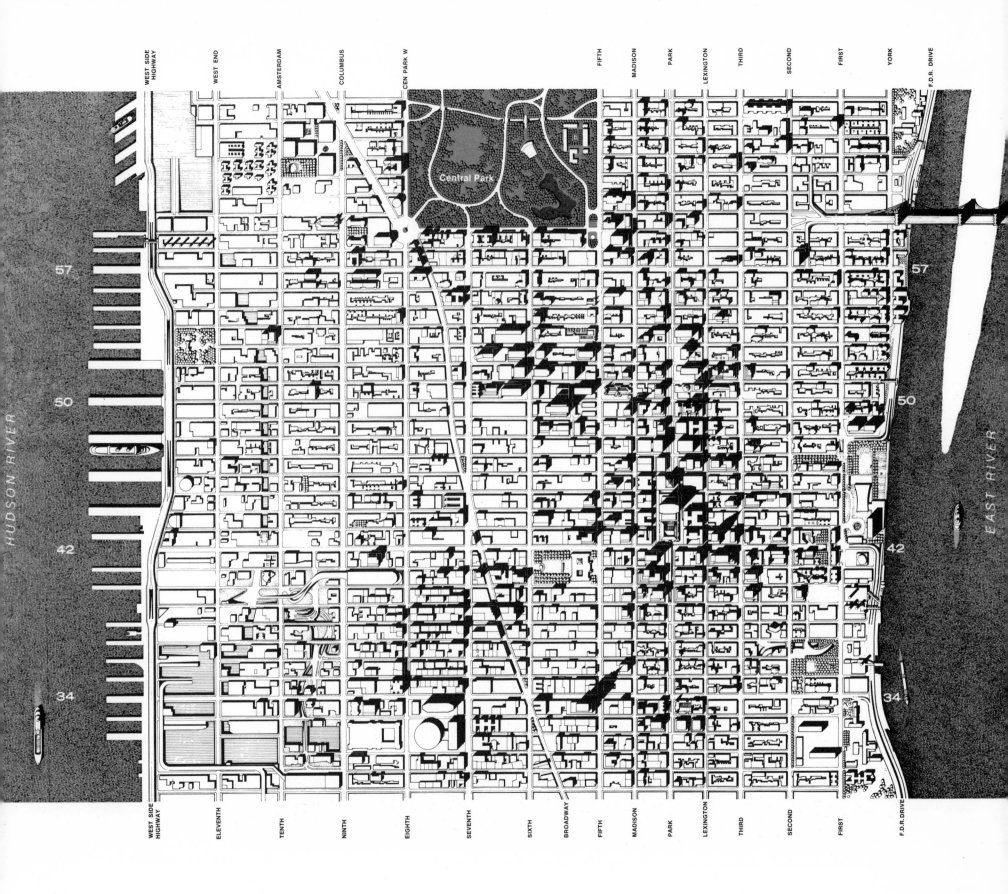

EXISTING PHYSICAL FORM: MIDTOWN MANHATTAN

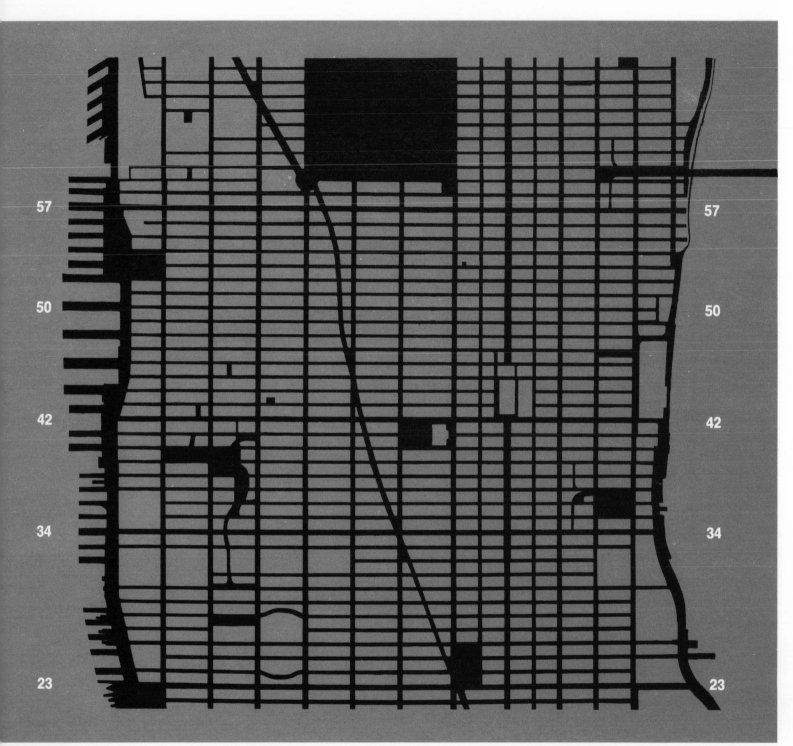

57

50

42

34

23

57

50

42

34

23

PUBLIC LAND OWNERSHIP
(left)

The pattern of publicly owned land—predominantly street rights-of-way and parks — has been historically the most permanent feature of any city plan. Despite small adjustments over time, such as in the vehicular tunnel approaches and the new superblocks along the periphery, the surface grid of Midtown basically remains as drawn in 1811. The permanence of street rights-of-way is reinforced by utilities and other "Access Tree roots" that follow them. It is into this infrastructure grid that a succession of private developments are "plugged in."

EXISTING GRAIN:
BUILT-UP AREA
(right)

The area covered by buildings at present is shown at right. Between the buildings and the public rights-of-way and parks is what may be called "private open space." It is rather extensive in the residential areas along the periphery, but almost non-existent, except for a few new office plazas, in the commercial center. The relatively low building coverage on the West Side points up opportunities for future growth.

existing buildings

pedestrian open space-parks, plazas, sidewalks

PUBLIC OWNERSHIP: MIDTOWN MANHATTAN

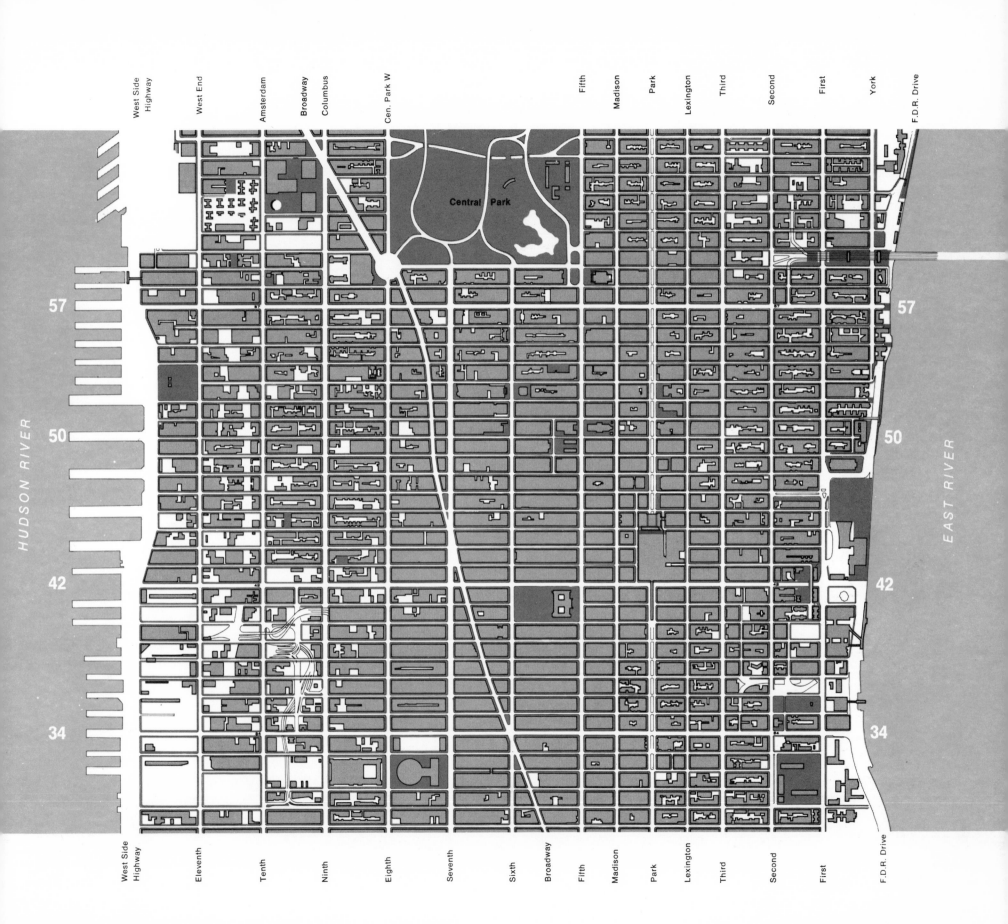

EXISTING GRAIN: BUILT FORM

Grand Central

Rockefeller Center

Garment District

FUNCTIONAL AREAS

The Manhattan CBD is a machine for bringing together a wide variety of talents and facilitating face-to-face communication. While many establishments in the CBD serve or draw upon persons working anywhere between Central Park and the Battery—as a corporate headquarters regularly uses or consults Madison Avenue advertising agencies, Wall Street financial experts, Valley printers, City Hall area government agencies and many more—establishments which do business together or share customers or services very frequently tend to locate together in the same neighborhood. Thus Midtown has become a congeries of functional clusters—the theater district, the garment center, the international area around the United Nations and many others. New development should complement rather than obstruct these functional groupings.

United Nations

Theater District

■ offices

■ regional shopping

■ theater-entertainment

■ international, public institutions

■ garment district

■ warehousing and distribution

■ residential

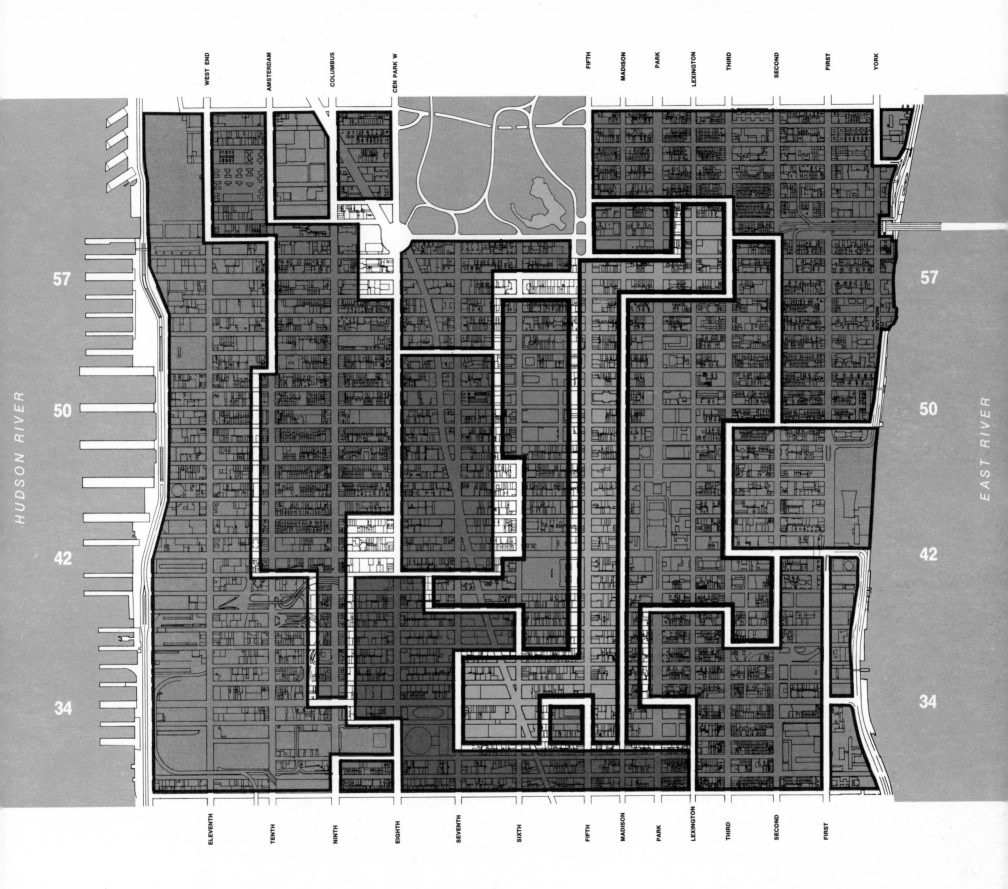

FUNCTIONAL AREAS DIAGRAM

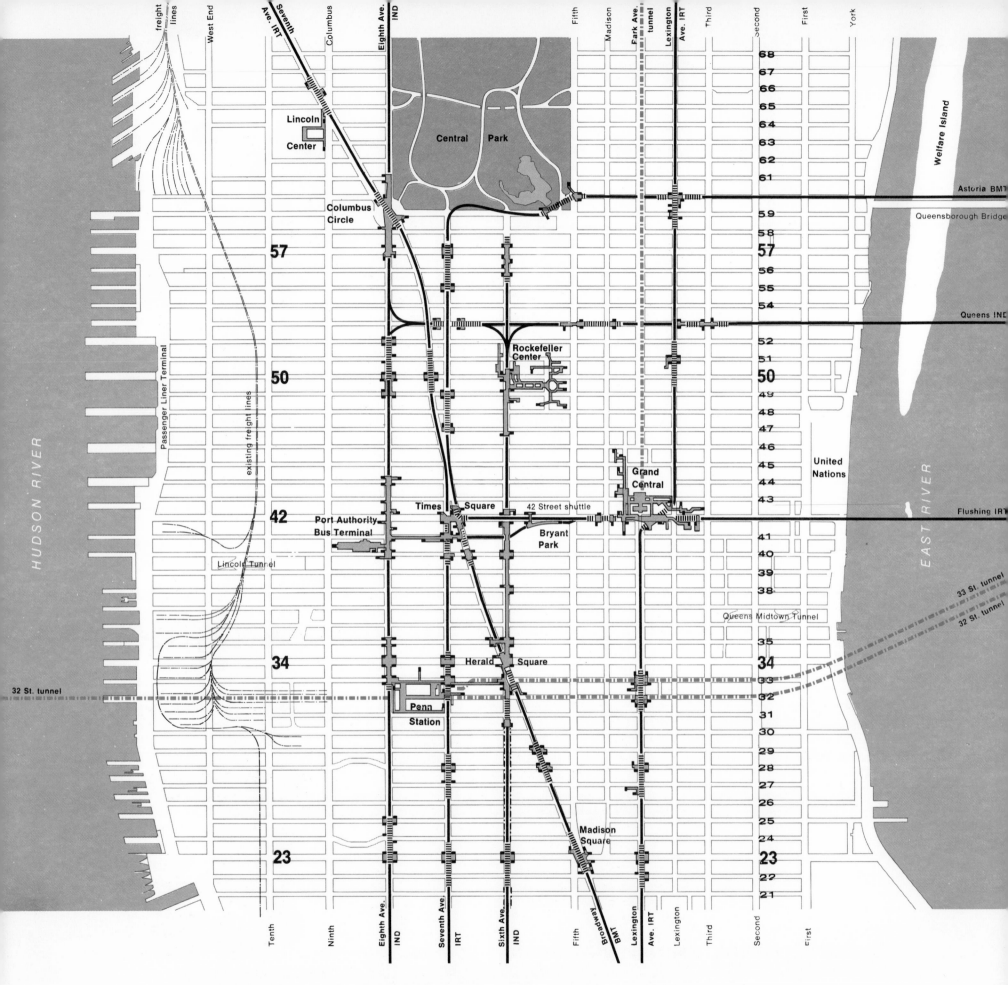

EXISTING MOVEMENT AND THE FIRST MEZZANINE LEVEL

EXISTING MOVEMENT
(left)

Existing public transit facilities are shown on this drawing, with the extensive mezzanine or first pedestrian concourse level (gold) one level below the ground but a level above the subway. Much of this mezzanine level is dark and poorly ventilated. However, reconstruction and new development could bring in light and fresh air, making it a vital and pleasant pedestrian level, freed from cross movements of cars and pedestrians that conflict at grade level. Notice that underground corridors from Grand Central and Rockefeller Center almost reach each other, symbolizing their strong relationship and the desire, as yet unrealized, to move directly between them. Though very rarely seen, such a map of Midtown is no less important than the conventional maps of the street surface.

first mezzanine level

—∎— commuter rail

▮▮▮▮▮ subway station platforms

HIGHEST HOUR VS. 24-HOUR STATION ENTRIES
(above right)

A high degree of accessibility at Grand Central, Penn Station and Times Square becomes evident in this diagram showing numbers of people passing through turnstiles at individual stations during the highest hour and in a 24-hour period. Station areas having a high peak hour use (red) but a relatively low 24 hour use (orange) reflect the daytime office type activities around these stations.

The one-way turnstile passenger counts at stations shown on the diagram are (in thousands):

	24 hrs.	highest hr.
Grand Central	149	49
Times Square	128	27
Herald Square	103	22
Penn Station, 7 Ave.	71	11
Bus Terminal, 8 Ave.	65	10
Rockefeller Center	57	12
Penn Station, 8 Ave.	57	11
59 St. Lex. Ave.	50	11
42 St. 6 Ave.	44	12
Columbus Circle	43	6
23 St. Park Ave.	35	9
51 St. Lex. Ave.	35	9
5 Ave. 53 St.	34	11
Lex. Ave. 53 St.	33	9
33 St. Park Ave.	26	7
23 St. 6 Ave.	26	10
50 St. Broadway	26	5
57 St. Broadway	25	7
28 St. Park Ave.	24	5
49 St. Broadway	22	6
23 St. Broadway	22	6
23 St. 8 Ave.	18	3
50 St. 8 Ave.	17	3
23 St. 7 Ave.	17	4
5 Ave. 42 St.	16	5
28 St. 7 Ave.	15	5
5 Ave. 60 St.	15	4
28 St. Broadway	12	5
7 Ave. 53 St.	12	3
66 St. Broadway	11	2

SPHERE OF INFLUENCE OF SUBWAY STATIONS
(below right)

The circles show areas within 700 feet of subway stations — roughly a three-minute walk. The red streets indicate how far one can actually walk in three minutes, following the rectangular street grid. This walking distance is a desirable determinant of office location.

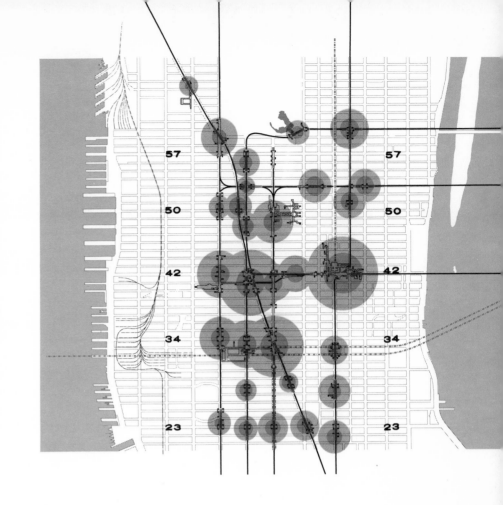

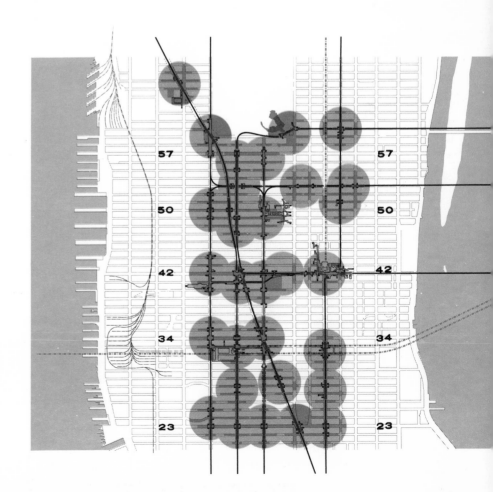

Office Projections

Midtown Manhattan should be prepared for additional office construction, during the next thirty-five years, equivalent to about 66 Time and Life buildings, eight Rockefeller Centers or eight World Trade Centers. This is about 400,000 office jobs, 80 percent of the increase in office employment projected for the entire Manhattan CBD.

Factors underlying this recommendation are:

1. Economic projections for the Region indicating a growth of about 1.4 million jobs in office buildings in the 31-county New York Region Study Area. (Regional Plan Association, **The Region's Growth,** May 1967.)

2. A finding that, of the total office jobs expected in the Region, a significant share will be headquarters types — related to over-all business policies of large organizations. These have traditionally favored the Manhattan CBD.

3. The determination that careful application of the functional, form and amenity principles described in the previous chapter would make possible the accommodation of these 400,000 more office workers in Midtown, without sacrificing efficiency, convenience or environmental quality.

4. The likelihood that this tremendous quantity of offices cannot be properly handled outside the CBD and finally, that the social needs of the Region require keeping a large number of jobs in the older cities. (See Regional Plan Association, **Jamaica Center,** April, 1968.)

Because one service-type job is usually required to support every five office-type jobs, about 80,000 additional workers must be provided for. An increase can also be expected in visitors for business, shopping and recreation purposes.

PROJECTED OFFICE GROWTH
(right)

New office space needed in Midtown Manhattan to accommodate some 400,000 additional office workers equals about 80 million net rentable square feet, symbolized here by 66 Time and Life buildings.

The Time and Life building is selected to illustrate the magnitude of projected office expansion in Midtown Manhattan. Built in 1959, it has 48 floors, and employs over 6,000 workers on 1,500,000 square feet of gross rentable office space. This is substantially more than the "average" post-war office building (which has 30 floors and somewhat over 500,000 square feet of rentable space) but is used here, because of distinctive size and coverage (half a large city block) as a symbol of the office space to be added. Future buildings will vary in size, of course, and are neither expected nor desired to be located in the diagrammatic arrangement on the map at right.

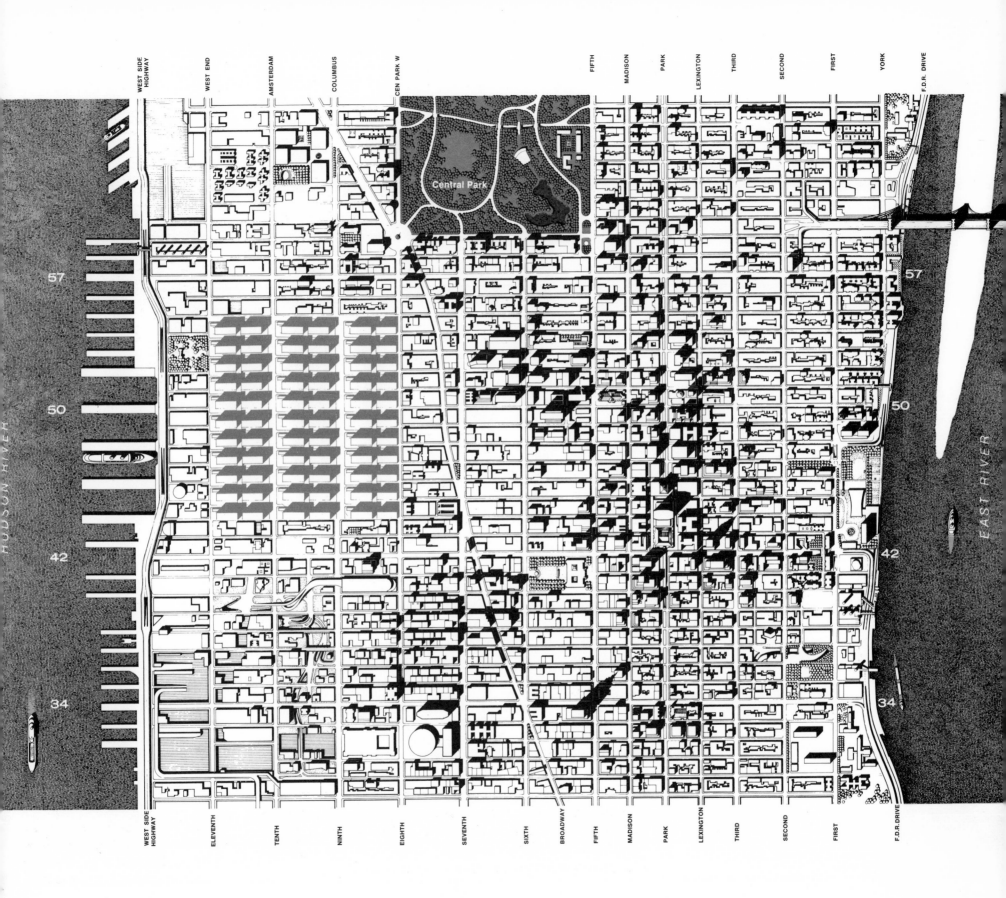

OFFICE PROJECTIONS DIAGRAM

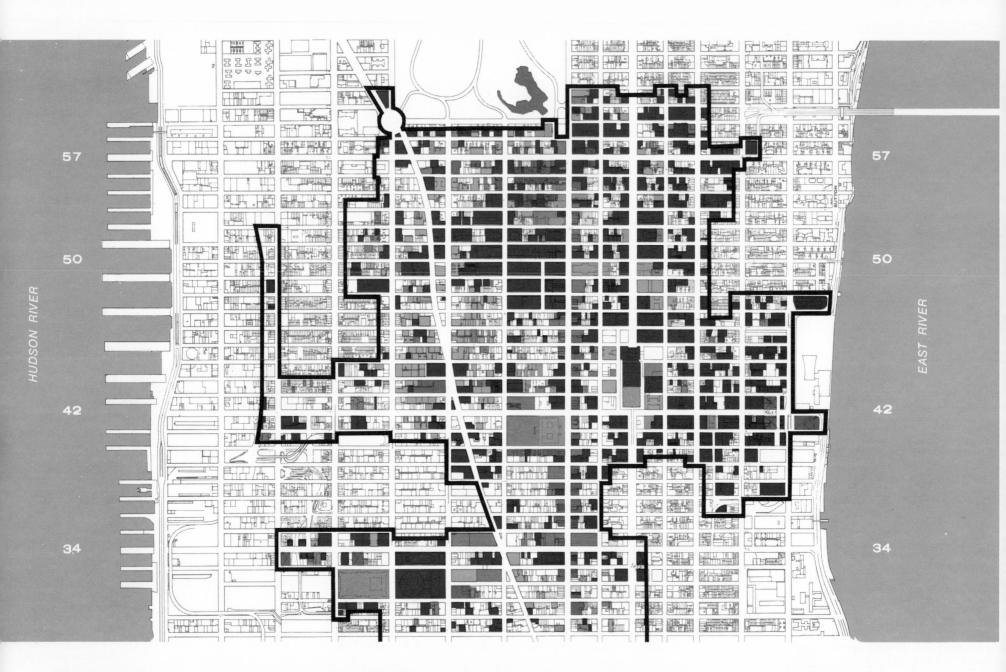

PERMANENT AREAS IN MIDTOWN COMMERCIAL DISTRICT

PLACES WHICH ARE MOST LIKELY TO REMAIN IN PRESENT USE AND PLACES WHICH SHOULD NOT BE CONSIDERED POTENTIAL OFFICE SITES

Given the projected number of new office buildings, where should they be located? Outlined above is the area in Midtown which is presently zoned to accommodate large office buildings. All of this area is in some use now, but some structures are clearly more resistant to change than others, and some should be made more resistant for social and amenity reasons. All colored parcels on the map are occupied by uses which are considered relatively permanent ("hard"). The first four categories shown in the legend are "hard" by fairly objective criteria: all post-1948 construction is expected to endure until the end of the century; major pre-war buildings, such as those of Rockefeller Center, the Chrysler Building and similar structures are also included in this category. Also considered objectively "hard" are important shopping districts, such as Fifth Avenue and Herald Square, as well as major institutions and officially-designated landmarks. The last two categories in the legend are "hard" for relatively subjective social and design reasons. These comprise theaters, clubs, hotels (mostly in the commercial entertainment district) as well as potential landmarks and intimate-scale buildings with specialty shops and restaurants which seem worth retaining despite their susceptibility to displacement with offices or other uses with a greater earning power.

Objective Criteria

- new construction *
- regional shopping
- parks and institutions
- landmarks

* post-war fireproof construction and certain large office buildings constructed in the 1930's.

Subjective Criteria

- Theaters, clubs, concert halls, hotels
- potential landmarks and appropriately-located specialty shops

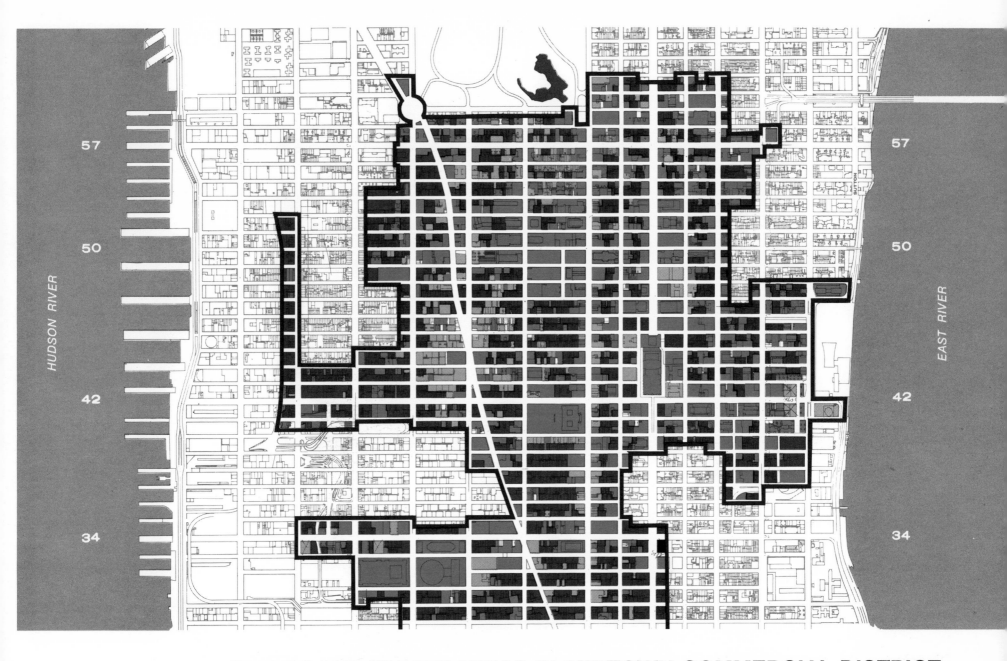

"HARD" AND "SOFT" AREAS IN MIDTOWN COMMERCIAL DISTRICT

PERMANENT PLACES AS CONTRASTED WITH IMPERMANENT AREAS SUBJECT TO DEVELOPMENT WITH OFFICE BUILDINGS

The parcels in areas which are not colored in the map on the opposite page contain uses considered impermanent, or "soft." These places are generally most available for development; on the map above, they are shown in blue. Most of Midtown is comprised of uses which seem to be or ought to be relatively permanent, as evidenced by the amount of red above. But there is a great deal of land which is subject to change. Theoretically, there is sufficient land capacity within the area zoned for offices to accommodate most of the projected growth. In practice, however, all the "soft" parcels shown above cannot be assembled for office buildings given present real estate practices, nor should they. Given the design goal of maintaining contrast between "high" and "low," certain areas, notably the theater district, should remain "low" despite the numerous "soft" parcels they contain. Moreover, as the map on the following page shows, much of the "soft" land is not in close proximity to subway stations. Priority in development should clearly go to the 'soft' sites with the greatest access potential.

"objective" permanence

"subjective" permanence

"soft" areas

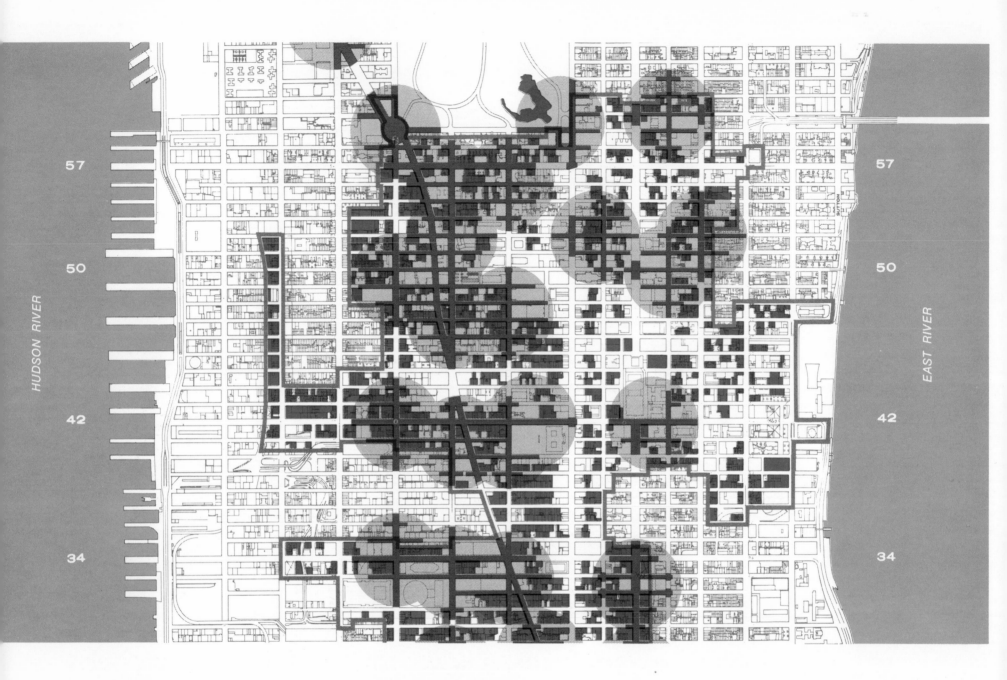

ACCESSIBILITY AS A FORM DETERMINANT

"SOFT" AREAS WITHIN A SHORT WALK OF SUBWAY STATIONS

Large buildings in which several thousand people work should be located within easy walking distance of rail and subway stations. The map above overlays the areas within a three-minute walk of subway stations, shown on page 69, on the map of "soft" or developable parcels shown on the previous page. The resulting areas of overlap are prime sites for the growing of "access trees" within the district presently zoned for office development. These are also priority sites for the implementation of development controls, described in Chapter 5. While adequate for the short to medium range, these sites, however, would not be able to accommodate all of the projected development. For the longer range, sites outside the presently-zoned Midtown office district will have to be sought.

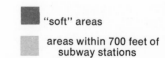

"soft" areas

areas within 700 feet of
subway stations

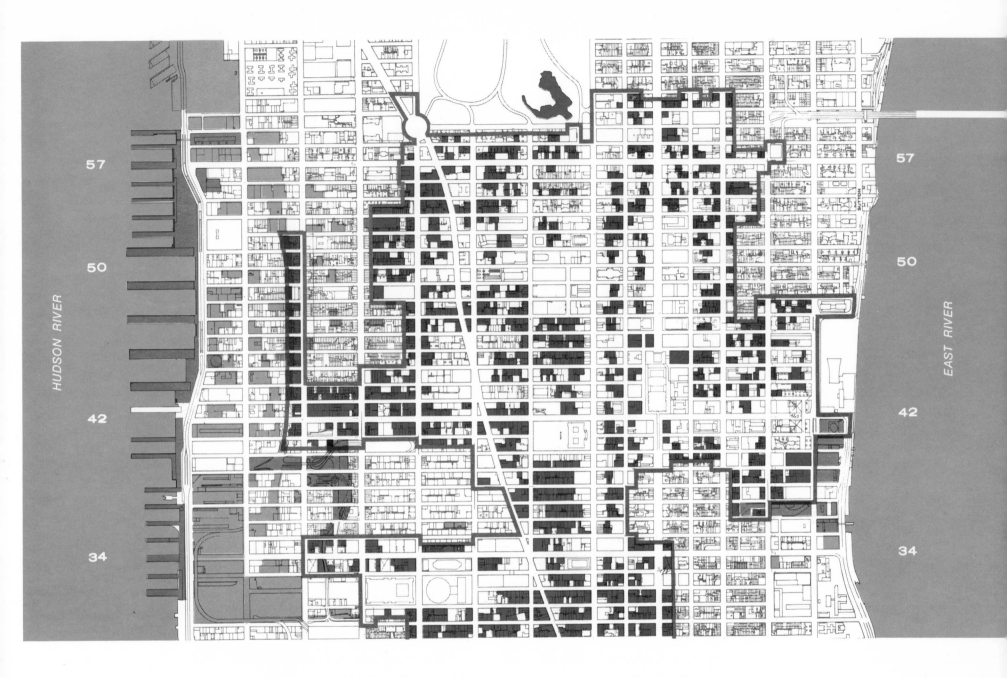

57

50

HUDSON RIVER

42

34

EAST RIVER

57

50

42

34

LAND ASSEMBLY AS A FORM DETERMINANT

PUBLICLY-KNOWN LAND OWNERSHIP

Land ownership within the presently-zoned Midtown commercial district is highly fractionalized. There are very few parcels of one-half acre or more of "soft" land within it that are publicly known to be in single ownership. The greatest concentration of large, developable parcels in single ownership is on the West Side toward the Hudson River, as the above map shows. On this basis, an expansion of the office district toward the Hudson River in the long range would seem to merit investigation. A future westward expansion of the Midtown CBD is, moreover, logical on transportation grounds. Any substantial increment to total CBD employment will require new rapid transit capacity beyond present programs. In view of the geography of Manhattan, the shortest path in and out of it is in an east-west direction. A new high-speed east-west line in Midtown would not only facilitate sorely inadequate crosstown movement and stimulate the commercial development of high-amenity water-front sites, but also focus residential development into nearby, but underutilized, areas to the east and west of Manhattan.

■ "Soft" land within present
  commercial district

  "Soft" land outside present
  commercial district

■ publicly-owned,
    in parcels over ½ acre

  privately owned,
    in parcels over ½ acre

73

The Conceptual Diagram

Midtown's conceptual organization is developed here from the functional and visual form principles discussed in Chapter 3, and in reference to the land use and transportation analysis presented on the previous pages. Clusters of high office towers centered on transportation access points are separated by "lows" in which restaurants, specialty shops, theaters, clubs and department stores are located.

Existing office clusters and possible locations for new clusters are shown in the diagram. Existing office "highs" can be identified: Grand Central Station, the Park Avenue strip, Rockefeller Center and Penn Station. Possible new office clusters would include one on the West Side, expansion and consolidation of Rockefeller Center westward to about Eighth Avenue and an extension of the Penn Station area.

High-density residential clusters are proposed at the four corners of Midtown. There is a tendency toward this pattern now.

Public open space envelopes the superliner terminal on the Hudson, and extends over and beyond the peripheral highways on both rivers.

A conceptual diagram is but one step toward superior urban design. It provides a form framework for the many small decisions which may then become a meaningful visual whole.

Pure compositional organization of urban forms and spaces is not the objective of this concept. Its primary objective is to achieve visual clarity, order and maximum amenity.

CONCEPTUAL DIAGRAM

"Lows" should be retained — on Fifth Avenue, which should remain a relatively sunlit shopping street, in the Times Square theater district, and at the southern edge of Central Park. Located around these, related to transit, would be the extensions of established office areas (such as Rockefeller Center and Penn Station) and new office centers. Housing would rise in the four corners, with parks along the rivers.

HIGHS

■ existing office clusters

■ future office expansion

■ major residential clusters (existing and future)

LOWS

■ existing shopping, hotel and entertainment districts

■ public open space

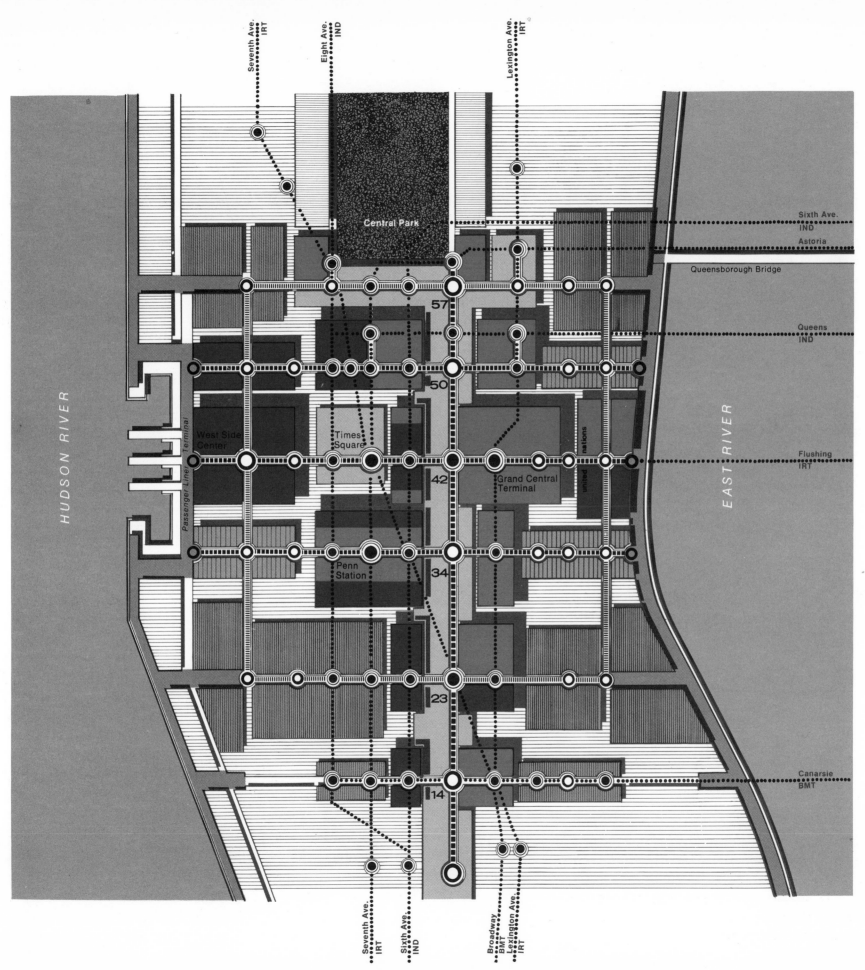

CONCEPTUAL DIAGRAM: MIDTOWN MANHATTAN

NEW MIDTOWN MOVEMENT

The circulation implications of employment growth projected to the year 2000 and beyond, and of substantially better environmental standards are far-reaching, and imply a large-scale reconstruction of the existing transportation infrastructure. This is important not only to get more workers to their jobs but also to allow easy interaction among them when they are there—the purpose of bringing so many persons to this compact center.

It has not been the intent of this study to develop a transportation plan for Midtown. Rather, the intent has been to indicate the new scale of public transportation facilities necessary, and to set up a general framework for demonstrating the application of design principles. A visual analysis of movement systems is intended to relate circulation to the physical form of the CBD.

While the orthogonal grid of surface streets in Manhattan is eminently legible and conducive to orientation, the underground rail and transit network, built piecemeal, is poorly related to it in large-scale geometry, and even worse at the smaller scale of station-to-surface "interfaces." Moreover, post-war building trends have increasingly moved development away from transit, with the result that 70 percent of the jobs in Midtown are east of Sixth Avenue, while 70 percent of transit capacity is west.

Future transit additions should clarify rather than further confuse the basic geometry of the transit network. Prior to locating new lines and stations, or new expressways visual analyses of the type illustrated on these pages have to be carried out; nodal stations on the existing system will have to be totally rebuilt to integrate the below-ground spaces with those above ground, and crosstown movement facilitated.

MODELS OF MOVEMENT SYSTEMS

Basic Delivery
(above right)
A schematic study sketch of the basic delivery systems in Midtown—existing and proposed railroads (dark blue), subways (light blue) and expressways (yellow) is shown.

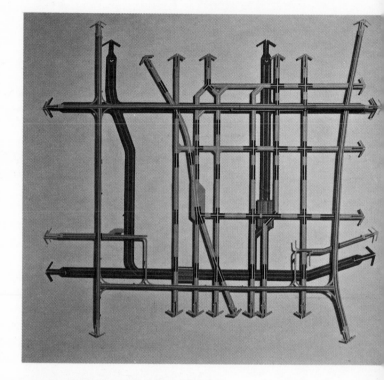

Pedestrian Interconnections
(below right)
Superimposed on it at the lower right is shown a study of major pedestrian interconnections, which could range from promenades along the waterfronts to mechanically aided pedestrian conveyances along selected crosstown streets, with collecting plazas at major terminals and stations.

Movement Systems Superimposed

The superimposition of all movement systems results in the three-dimensional study model on the right. This graphic construction shows the relative vertical alignment of the horizontal movement systems. The model was used to study the complexities of the existing situation and to test the addition of new lines.

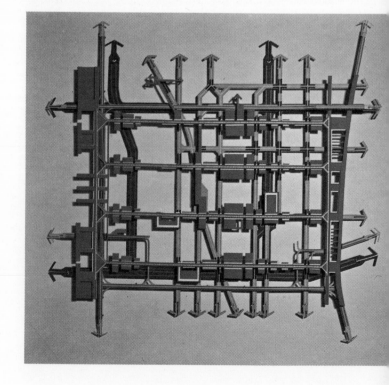

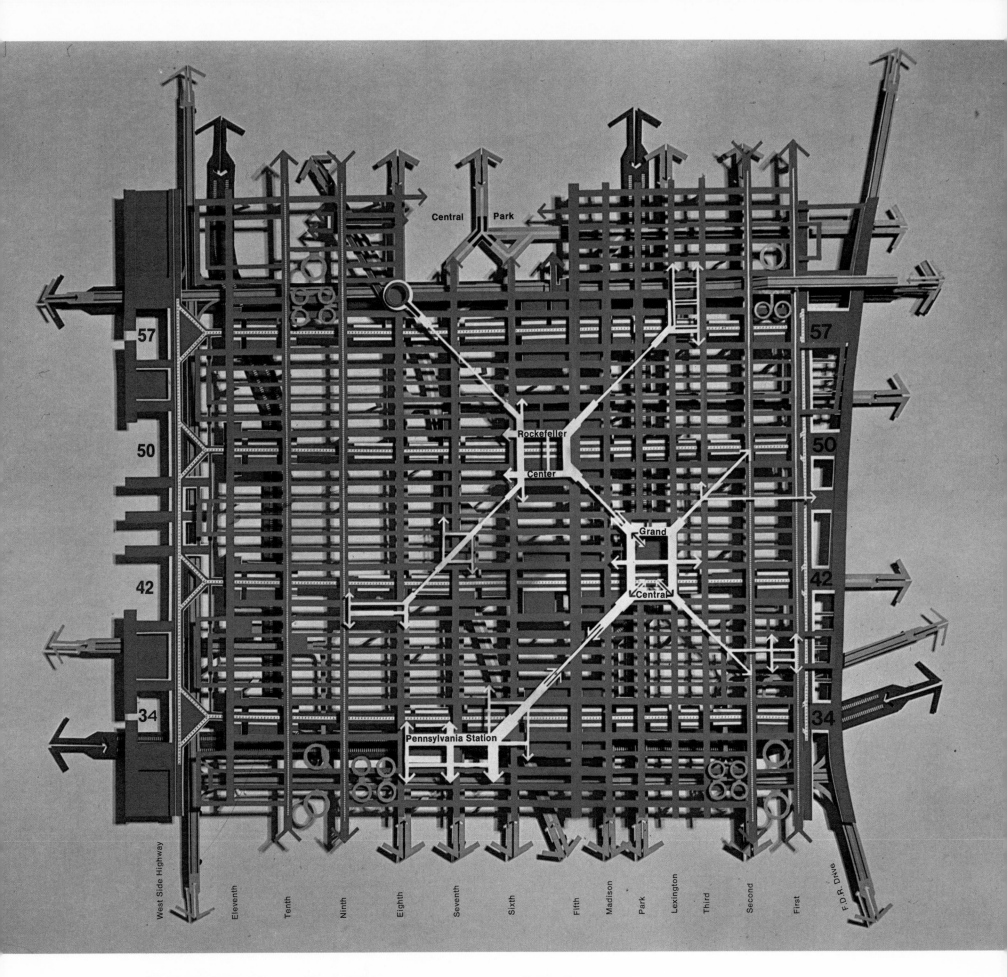

Central Park

Rockefeller Center

Grand Central

Pennsylvania Station

57

50

42

34

57

50

42

34

West Side Highway

Eleventh

Tenth

Ninth

Eighth

Seventh

Sixth

Fifth

Madison

Park

Lexington

Third

Second

First

F.D.R. Drive

MOVEMENT SYSTEMS ANALYSIS MODEL

77

Mass Movement Systems

Analyzing the change over time of public transportation facilities helps to predict and guide the future form implications inherent in new movement systems.

These diagrams show stages in the development of possible future transit over the next decades.

Solid lines indicate the present system; dashed lines signify future service of different types—not only subway extensions and commuter rail additions but technologically advanced, high-speed, high-capacity systems and new types of shuttle facilities for crosstown movements. New development on the West Side would occur only after the provision of new access there.

— Proposed Second Avenue subway with connections to the Bronx and to Queens.

— Commuter rail connection from the proposed 63rd Street tunnel between Manhattan and Queens into the Grand Central and Penn Station as well as a tie-in from the West Side Penn-Central freight line into Penn Station.

— New river-to-river east-west shuttles 34th, 42nd, 50th and 57th Streets.

— A new east-west transit line is proposed to increase peak-hour capacity to the CBD as the number of jobs rises. This is expected to be a radically advanced system, probably based on the principle of pendulum movement (allowing far faster acceleration and deceleration than horizontal transit lines can provide comfortably), which is important for close station-spacing, and incorporating gravity and a vacuum as motive and braking forces. Such a new and very much faster transit technology probably can be operational within ten to fifteen years, when the added capacity will be needed.

— In the longer range, two north-south routes based on the same technology, more than doubling the speed of

STAGE 1 (existing)

STAGE 2

STAGE 3

STAGE 4

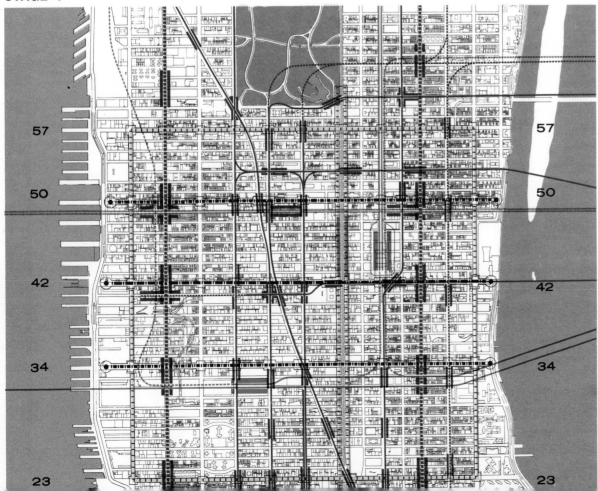

movement northward toward the Bronx and southward toward Staten Island and Brooklyn.

— A shoppers' shuttle at grade, relatively slow but frequent or continuous and with frequent or continuous opportunity to enter or leave, is proposed for Fifth Avenue, with an east-west tail to Herald Square at the south and to Lexington Avenue and 59th Street on the north.

— New pedestrianways north and south between avenues, illustrated here somewhat randomly, located between Fifth and Sixth Avenues.

— Major new pedestrian open space along the rebuilt superliner pier area extending north and south, as well as along the East River's edge.

— Subway platforms and concourses opened to light and air, and much greater interest and amenity on the underground levels.

— Glass arcades over certain special streets and interchange spaces, and all-weather climatization for dense shopping districts.

metropolitan subways

commuter and regional rail

crosstown shuttles

gravity vacuum tube

mechanically aided pedestrian systems

Individual Movement Systems

Though the central business district must remain compact to achieve its function of easy face-to-face communication among very large numbers of people, and though individual movement systems — today, the automobile and taxicab — occupy too much space to allow as much use in the CBD as many people would wish, some provision must be made for private vehicles, as well as for delivery trucks and similar service vehicles which comprise a very substantial portion of the street traffic in Manhattan.

Autos should, on the whole, be kept outside the CBD, stored on the perimeter at points of easy direct access to intra-CBD circulation systems so people can get out of their cars and into the mass movement system.

For individual travel within the CBD, non-polluting, silent, small vehicles may eventually be developed, available to all within the CBD just as taxicabs now are, perhaps rented on a coin-in-the-slot basis.

Even before this comes about, faster auto and truck movement and more and pleasanter pedestrian space can be provided by a reorganization and reclassification of the existing gridiron.

— Tunnels across Manhattan under 29th-30th Streets, connecting the Lincoln to the Queens-Midtown Tunnel, and the West Side Highway to the Queensboro Bridge near 59th Street. With six lanes each, these could move as much traffic as now moves on two 100-foot-wide streets (like 34th and 42nd) **and** sixteen standard 60-foot-wide streets. The possibility is opened, then, of providing more space for pedestrians or other uses.

— Four pedestrian-oriented east-west streets with mechanical shuttles and little or no auto or taxi traffic, full

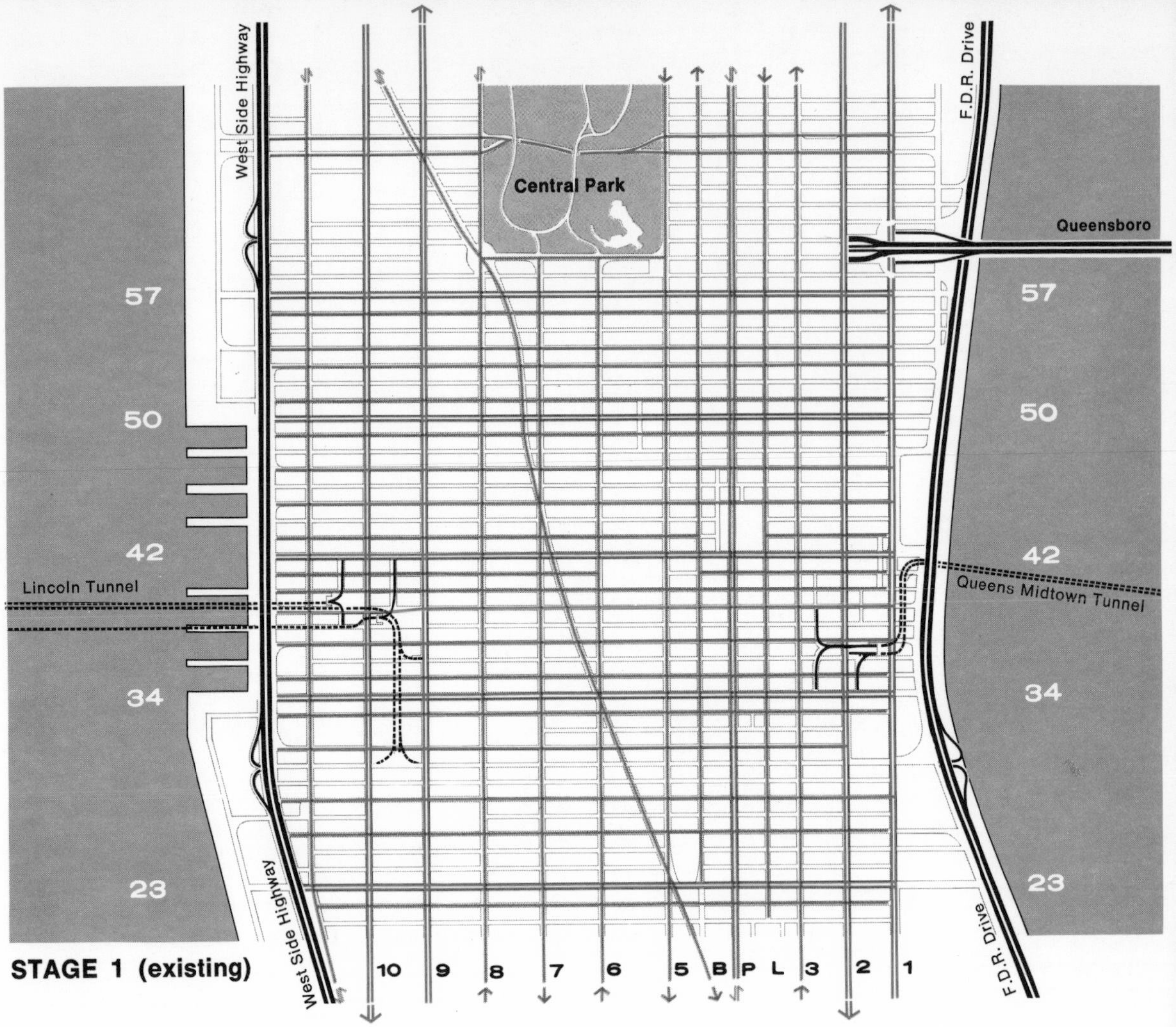

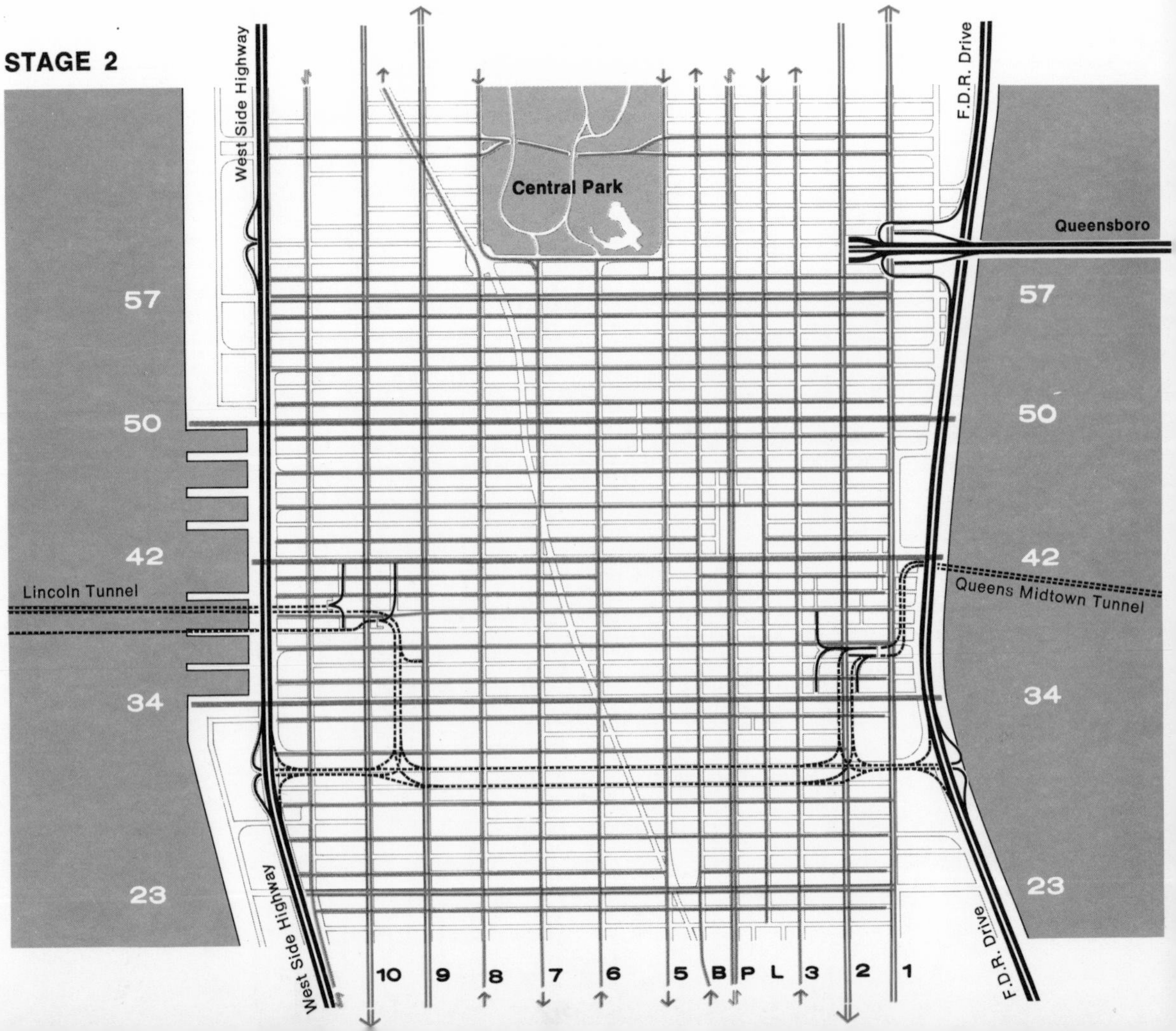

STAGE 1 (existing)

STAGE 2

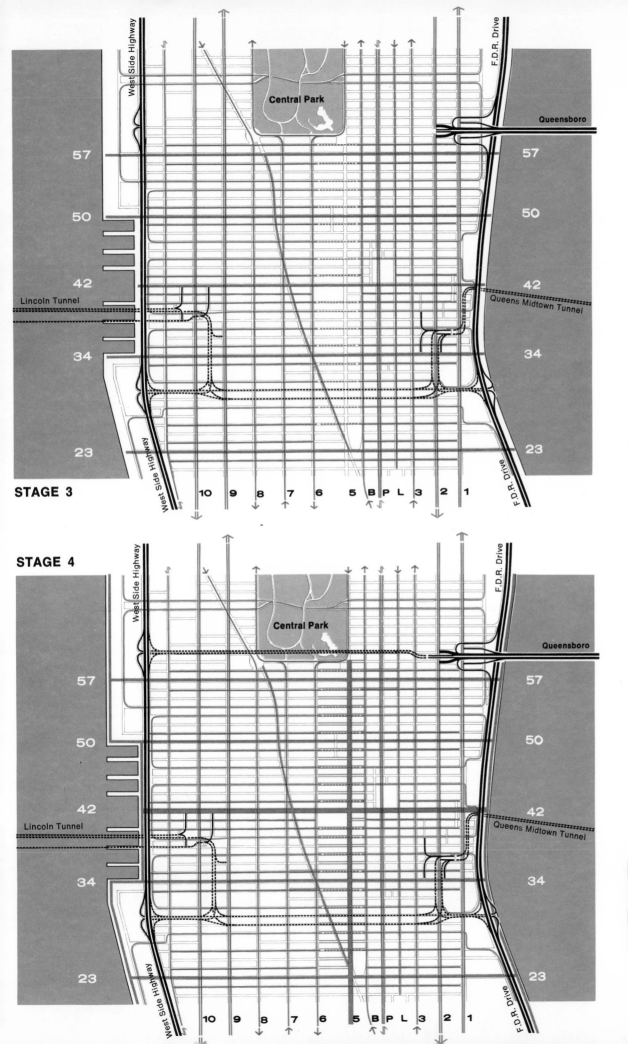

STAGE 3

STAGE 4

grade separation at intersections where feasible and heavy landscape treatment: 34th, 42nd, 50th and 57th.

— Two pedestrian-oriented north-south streets — Fifth Avenue and Broadway, closed to all but bus traffic in sections, with heavy landscape treatment.

— Structural, traffic and land use controls to encourage the functional specialization of the remaining street system into several classes:

a) Secondary, pedestrian-oriented east-west streets without truckbays and parking garages.

b) East-west service streets — little pedestrian traffic, primarily for autos and service vehicles.

c) North-south arterials — primarily autos and service vehicles, minimum pedestrian traffic: Ninth and Tenth Avenues, First and Second Avenues.

d) North-south standard avenues — limited service vehicles, primarily autos, taxis, and buses; high quality pedestrian amenity: Third, Lexington, Madison Avenues; Sixth, Seventh and Eighth Avenues.

e) Two north-south service avenues — totally service vehicles or access to parking facilities, storage and warehousing: Eleventh and Twelfth Avenues.

— Policies on the location of parking garages (out of the high-density areas) and on the provision of off-street truck loading docks (especially in manufacturing areas that are to stay) must complement any comprehensive surface circulation policy.

◼ limited access highways and tunnels

▨ arterial couplets , collector streets

▨ local streets

▨ pedestrian oriented streets

Composite Movement Systems

Shown at the right is an x-ray view of the multi-level complexity of all movement layers in Midtown. The public transportation is at the lower levels, with pedestrian sub-systems delineated above, below and at street grade.

Movement systems in the form indicated would provide reasonable standards of circulation and amenity within the CBD and of transportation capacity to the CBD for the projected number of CBD employees—standards suited to the high incomes and therefore high expectations that people will have by the year 2000 and beyond.

It is assumed that new technology will be enlisted in this improved transportation system, including transit powered by gravity and vacuum and mechanical aids to pedestrian movement, such as moving belts or quick-access shuttle vehicles. These devices almost surely will become available by the end of the century to meet the demand of the most influential business center in the world.

In the meantime, an improved organization for traffic to provide more efficient automobile movement in the CBD while giving pedestrians more space and more pleasure can be implemented in stages.

The resulting proposal for future movement systems is built upon the principles of form and function discussed earlier and on the existing form and movement systems of the CBD.

The diagonal pedestrian ways between major office clusters, both existing and proposed, and other modes of high-density pedestrian activity are not firmly proposed routes. They symbolize the emerging need for such pedestrian paths. The diagonal system is conceived as a high-efficiency, primarily utilitarian element to accommodate peak pedestrian movement. Ideally, it should be above ground, but the pattern of ownership and use and the negative aspects of total clearance and redevelopment in many districts make this very difficult. It would be easiest to achieve at new transit nodes or areas susceptible to total redevelopment. Underground portions would be short and opened to light and air at periodic intervals.

DIAGRAM OF COMPOSITE MOVEMENT SYSTEMS, PRESENT AND PROPOSED

This drawing helps in discerning where major transportation systems come together now and where they might occur in the future. It is a tool for determining the places to apply the Access Tree principle and where to invest in public infrastructure. It also illustrates the importance of the major crosstown movements.

- **····** crosstown shuttles
- metropolitan subways
- gravity vacuum tube
- commuter and regional rail
- pedestrian second level
- pedestrian on grade level
- pedestrian mezzanine level
- public open space

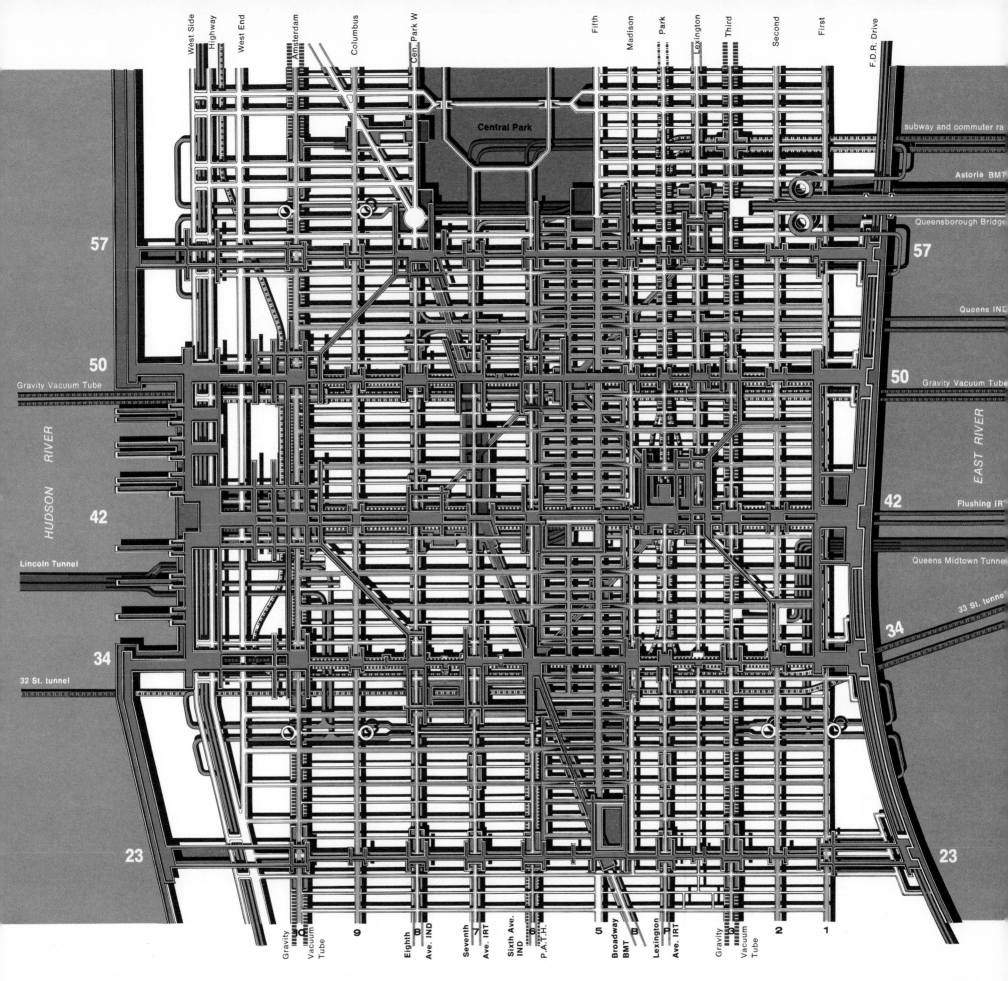

LONG RANGE MASS AND INDIVIDUAL MOVEMENT SYSTEMS

83

Form Response Diagram

This diagram is a direct response to the preceding long-range movement system's organization. It is intended to portray the form consequences as a diagram and not as a physical plan. It illustrates the application of the principles, based on a given movement systems organization. The principles behind the proposed movement systems could be carried out in several different ways, and if the details of that system varied from what is proposed here, the form response would, of course, vary from this diagram.

High-intensity uses (mainly office towers) would locate in large clusters at points of maximum accessibility to the CBD. While "lows" would be easily reached from these large clusters via secondary movement systems (which would provide relatively frequent and convenient internal CBD circulation), these points of secondary accessibility would not compete with high buildings.

With improved crosstown shuttles, the rivers could be used for the enjoyment of Midtown workers during lunchtime and after work, and the housing in the four corners of Midtown could offer, in addition to the amenity of the rivers, access advantages commensurate with proximity. This is not now the case because crosstown transportation is poor.

In a diagrammatic way (the gold color in the drawing), places are shown where the street and sidewalk surfaces would be punctured to bring light and air to the underground circulation level. The below-ground plazas or "mixing chambers" occur at important intersections of existing and future mass transit lines, as derived from the composite movement systems diagram on page 83.

DIAGRAMMATIC FORM RESPONSE

This diagram is intended to convey the bulk or forms which the long-range movement system could generate if the function, form, and amenity principles of Chapter Three were applied in midtown. The asphalt membrane of the street level would be penetrated to bring light and air into the special sub-surface "mixing chambers" (shown in gold). Reclaimed waterfronts for public recreation is shown in green.

This is a more detailed study of prospective physical form than the earlier conceptual diagram, but it is nevertheless a diagram and not a physical plan.

mezzanine open to light and air

public open space

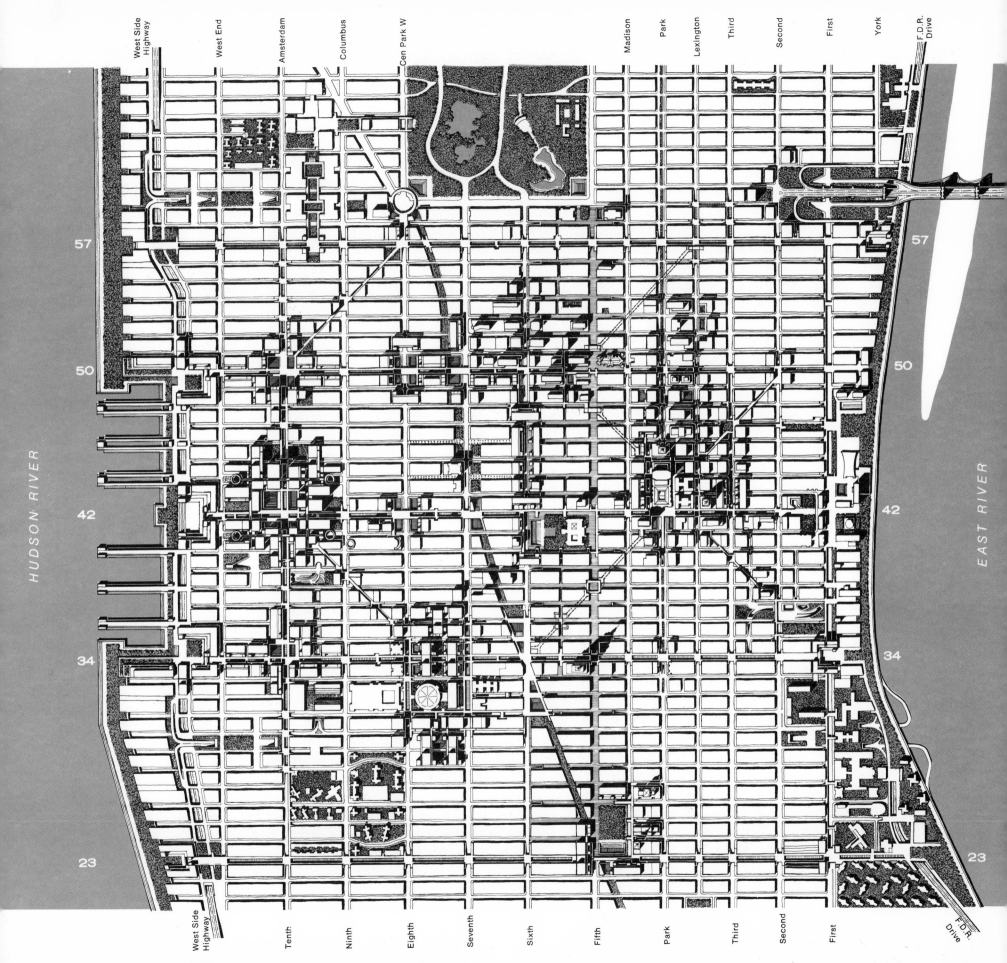

FORM RESPONSE DIAGRAM

FORTY-SECOND STREET: A CASE STUDY

A scale for illustrating the application of urban design principles smaller than that of Midtown is the scale of a single, distinctive street.

A case study of Forty-Second Street from river to river shows the present relationship of highs and lows and the variety in the types of clusters that make up Midtown. With this case study, the form response to proposed changes in the movement system can be shown in detail.

From an urban design point of view, Forty-Second Street and other special streets such as Fifth Avenue, are significant exceptions to the cluster concept. As linear elements they cross or, in the case of Forty-Second Street, link several of the nodes or clusters hypothesized as the basic physical module of Midtown. Fifth Avenue, in its role as a major circulation element, is a kind of linear shopping center and an important "low" in terms of form. In compari-

son, Forty-Second Street connects several separate Midtown districts, which are now almost internationally imageable, and which, collectively, mean Manhattan to many people.

Each area linked by Forty-Second Street has distinct traits. The United Nations district contains the headquarters of many international or related institutions. The Grand Central area contains the headquarters of many major corporations. The commercial-entertainment area of Times Square, including the theater district, bars, dance halls, movies, hotels and restaurants, is an international symbol of New York. Just to the south is the garment center where the emphasis is shifting from manufacturing to design, display, management and sales. The western edge is used today for warehousing and light manufacturing, with the passenger liner terminal along the Hudson waterfront.

FORTY-SECOND STREET

The entire street, river to river, may be regarded as an urban megastructure and is defined by continuity of movement, the interconnections of its activities, and its popular impression as a unit. In a sense, it is a single long building, four blocks wide and fourteen blocks long, with urban "rooms" attached to the central corridor. The "rooms" may be spaces such as Bryant Park, the United Nations Plaza or Times Square, or a special corridor such as the Fifth Avenue shopping spine.

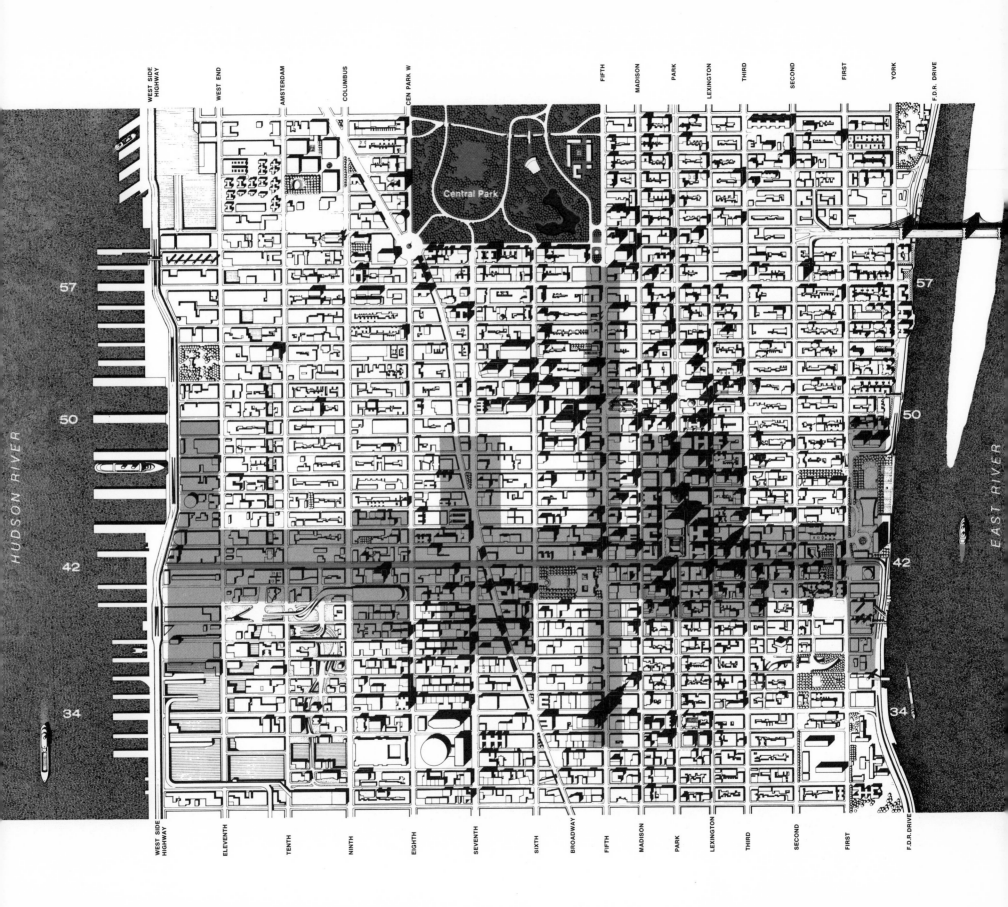

WEST SIDE HIGHWAY · WEST END · AMSTERDAM · COLUMBUS · CEN PARK W · FIFTH · MADISON · PARK · LEXINGTON · THIRD · SECOND · FIRST · YORK · F.D.R. DRIVE

57

50

42

34

Central Park

57

50

42

34

WEST SIDE HIGHWAY · ELEVENTH · TENTH · NINTH · EIGHTH · SEVENTH · SIXTH · BROADWAY · FIFTH · MADISON · PARK · LEXINGTON · THIRD · SECOND · FIRST · F.D.R. DRIVE

FORTY-SECOND STREET

1

2

EAST SIDE

3

4

FORTY-SECOND STREET

Forty-Second Street is a linear spine that links diverse concentrations or "nodes" of activity and connects the several spaces that are rather like large outdoor rooms. In some ways it is a prototype of the crosstown pedestrian axes whose reinforcement this study advocates. Typical views along it are shown on these pages.

1. United Nations Plaza—an "urban room" near the waterfront.

2. The 42nd Street "corridor"—westward view from the overpass at Tudor Place, with the Ford Foundation building on the right.

5

6

WEST SIDE

3. The vehicular overpass in front of Grand Central Terminal.
4. The central "urban room" — Bryant Park, with the re-surfaced Times Tower (now Allied Chemical Building) in the background.
5. Rathole-like stairways, about four feet wide, are now the only link between the underground subway world and the world above ground.
6. The movie theater section west of Times Suare.
7. A non-descript section farther west.
8. The non-descript end on the Hudson River.

7

8

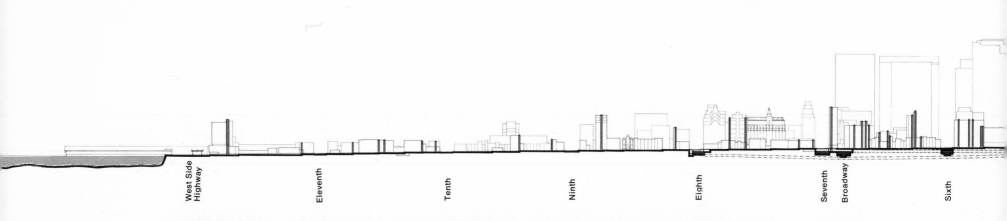

West Side Highway · Eleventh · Tenth · Ninth · Eighth · Seventh · Broadway · Sixth

EXISTING VERTICAL MOVEMENT ALONG FORTY-SECOND STREET

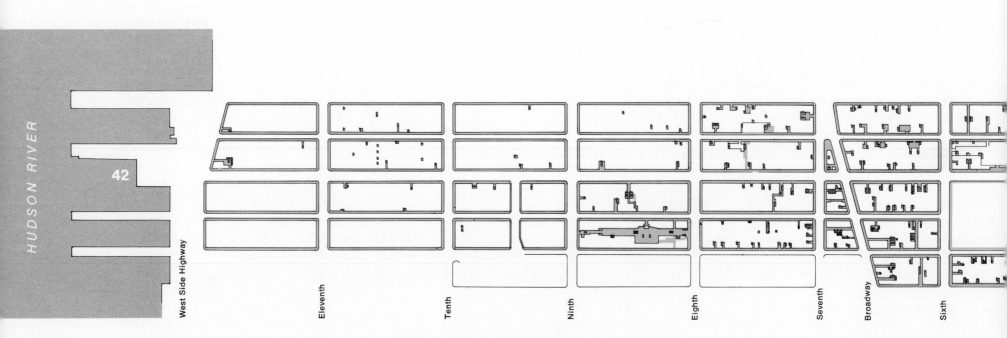

HUDSON RIVER

42

West Side Highway · Eleventh · Tenth · Ninth · Eighth · Seventh · Broadway · Sixth

EXISTING PUBLIC AND SEMI-PUBLIC PEDESTRIAN SPACE AT GRADE

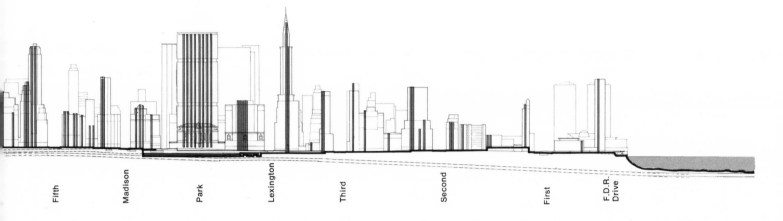

Fifth Madison Park Lexington Third Second First F.D.R. Drive

PEDESTRIAN SPACE FOR MOVEMENT: GRADE LEVEL
(left)

Large amounts of street level space are required for the circulation of pedestrians in Midtown's areas of high accessibility and high job density. Much of this space (orange) is inside private buildings, in lobbies and passageways that are needed, not only to serve elevators of individual buildings, but to supplement inadequate public sidewalks. As the lower diagram shows, sidewalks are uniform. But in the Grand Central vicinity, where the foot traffic is heavy, the ground floor of many buildings is given over to public or semi-public space for "horizontal" pedestrian movement.

The upper diagram indicates concentrations of elevators, or "vertical" movement systems, which rise from off-street lobbies. It further illustrates the extent to which elevators naturally cluster around major transportation interchanges.

Fifth Madison Park Lexington Third Second First F.D.R. Drive

EAST RIVER

42

■ vertical movement — elevators

□ public and semi-public open space at grade

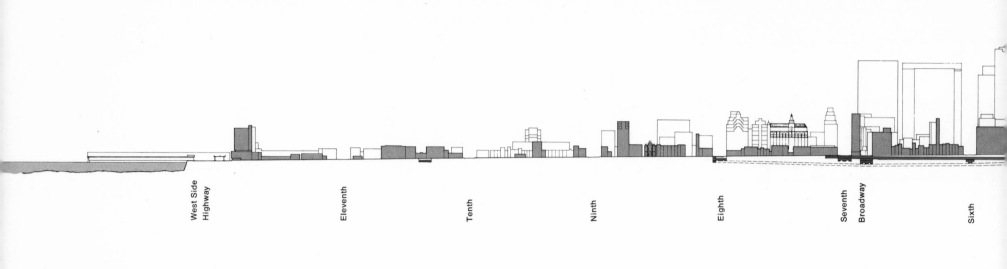

West Side
Highway

Eleventh

Tenth

Ninth

Eighth

Seventh

Broadway

Sixth

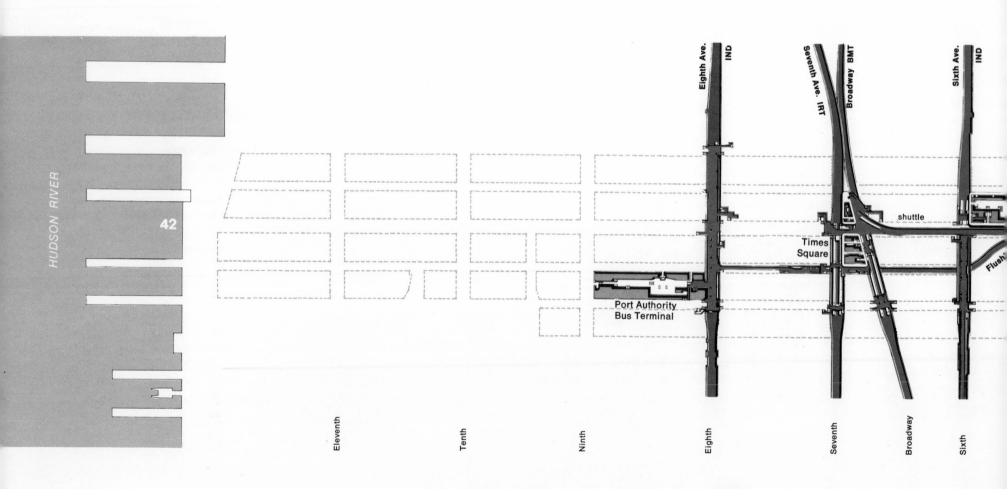

HUDSON RIVER

42

Eighth Ave.

IND

Seventh Ave. IRT

Broadway BMT

Sixth Ave.

IND

shuttle

Times
Square

Flush

Port Authority
Bus Terminal

Eleventh

Tenth

Ninth

Eighth

Seventh

Broadway

Sixth

EXISTING VERTICAL AND HORIZONTAL MOVEMENT SYSTEMS ALONG FORTY

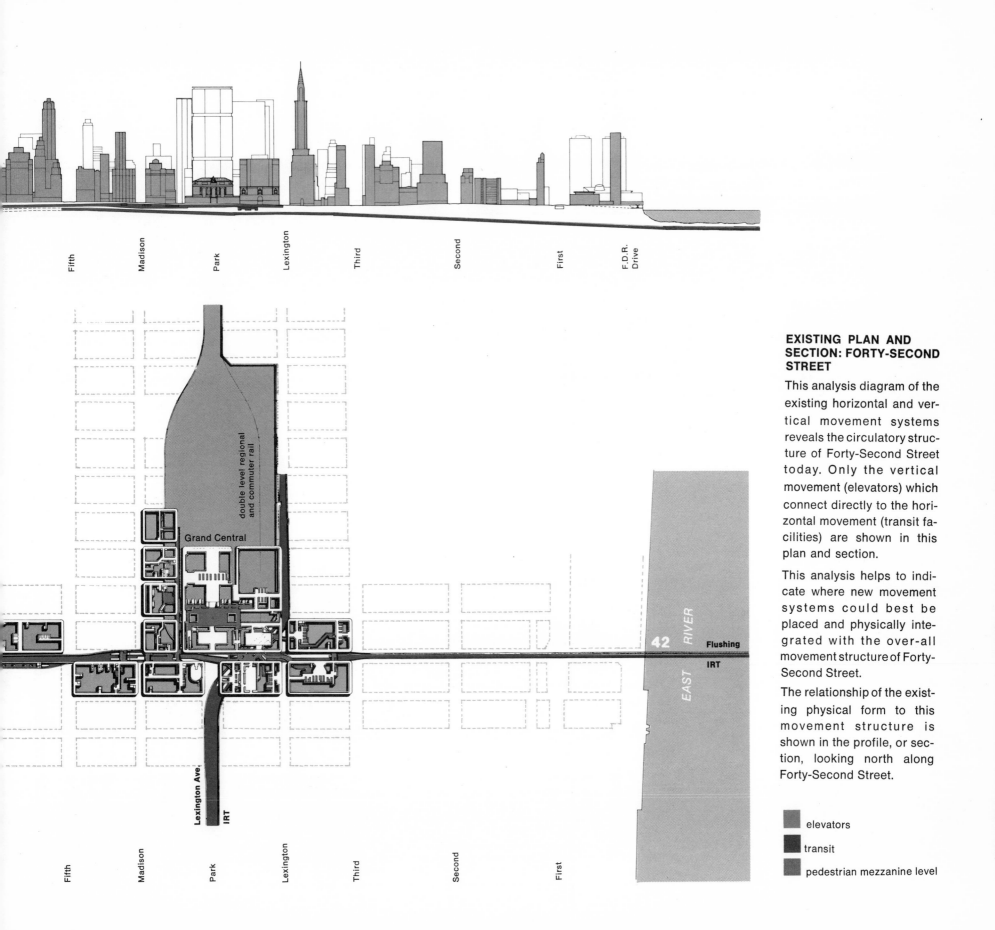

Fifth
Madison
Park
Lexington
Third
Second
First
F.D.R. Drive

double level regional and commuter rail

Grand Central

Lexington Ave. IRT

42

EAST RIVER

Flushing

IRT

Fifth
Madison
Park
Lexington
Third
Second
First

EXISTING PLAN AND SECTION: FORTY-SECOND STREET

This analysis diagram of the existing horizontal and vertical movement systems reveals the circulatory structure of Forty-Second Street today. Only the vertical movement (elevators) which connect directly to the horizontal movement (transit facilities) are shown in this plan and section.

This analysis helps to indicate where new movement systems could best be placed and physically integrated with the over-all movement structure of Forty-Second Street.

The relationship of the existing physical form to this movement structure is shown in the profile, or section, looking north along Forty-Second Street.

▮ elevators

▮ transit

▮ pedestrian mezzanine level

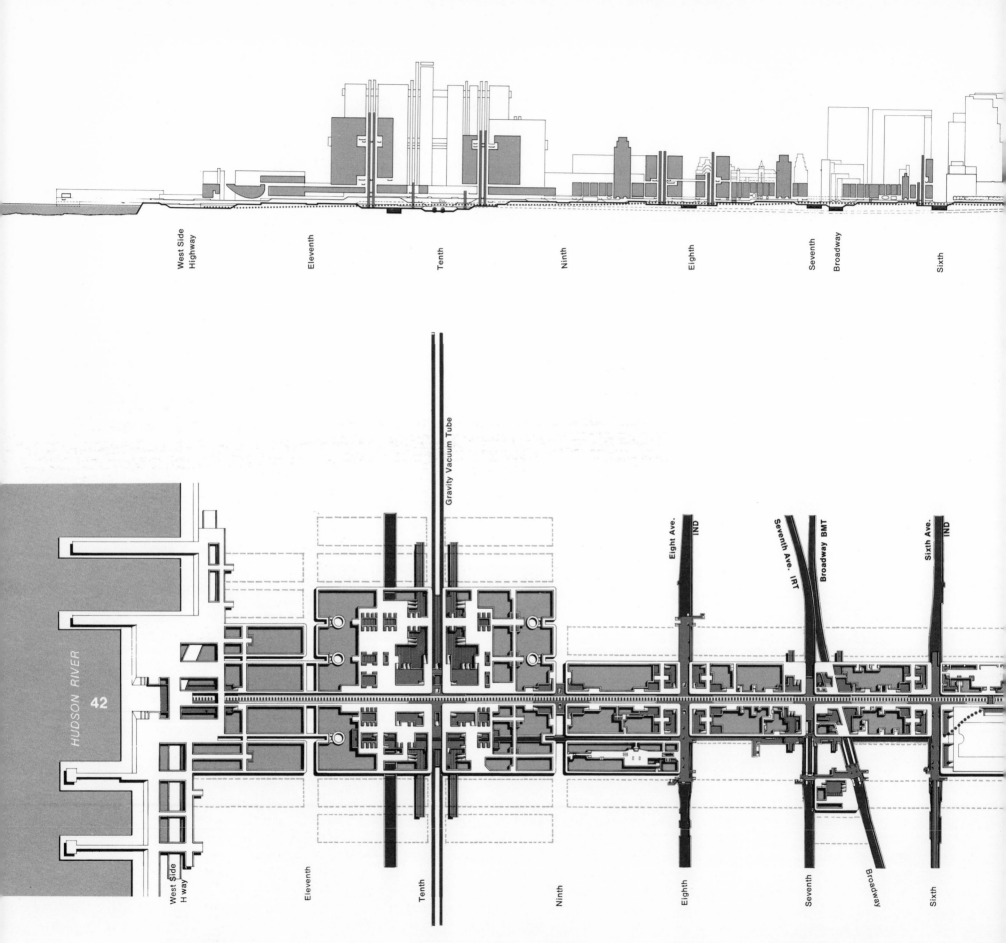

West Side Highway · Eleventh · Tenth · Ninth · Eighth · Seventh · Broadway · Sixth

HUDSON RIVER

42

Gravity Vacuum Tube

Eight Ave. IND · Seventh Ave. IRT · Broadway BMT · Sixth Ave. IND

West Side H'way · Eleventh · Tenth · Ninth · Eighth · Seventh · Broadway · Sixth

POSSIBLE VERTICAL AND HORIZONTAL MOVEMENT SYSTEMS ALONG FORTY

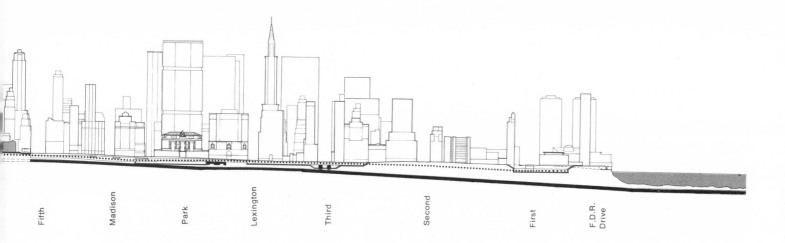

If movement along Forty-Second Street were changed by:

— A mechanical aid to pedestrian circulation, such as a moving belt or new type of shuttle train.

— Continuation of the Flushing line to the Hudson River;

And if other movement changes affecting Forty-Second Street were instituted:

— Very high-speed north-south transit lines along Tenth and Third Avenues. (This north-south movement along Third Avenue might, with further study, be relocated along Madison Avenue.)

— An auto-truck tunnel under 29th and 30th Streets, diverting a tremendous volume of crosstown traffic, much of it from Forty-Second Street.

— A northern exit from Grand Central Station, freeing that part of Forty-Second Street from a large peak-hour pedestrian load, and

— Better linkages of vertical and horizontal transportation;

Then the form of 42nd Street might respond as shown by the section and plan on the right. The most striking changes visible at this scale are the large office cluster centered on Tenth Avenue and a smaller cluster that would respond to new north-south transit hypothesized on Third Avenue. Also shown is the proposed passenger liner terminal and pedestrian area on the Hudson River.

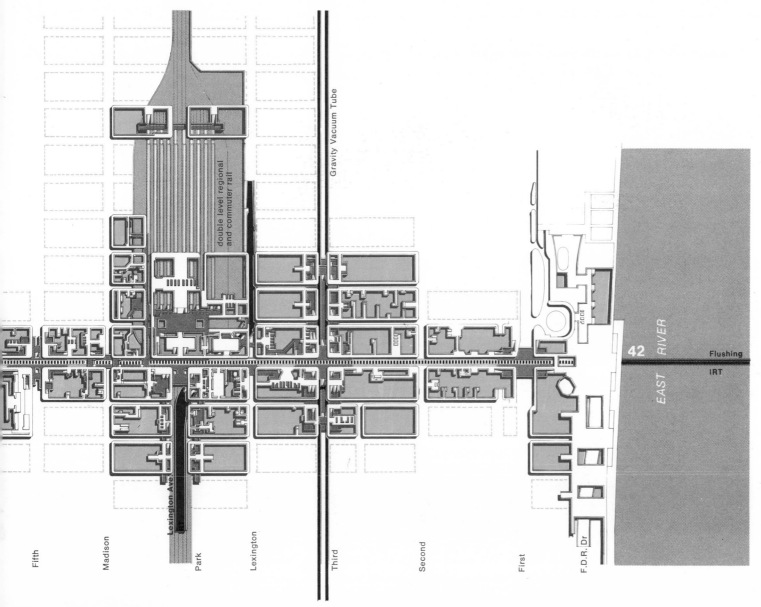

■ elevators

■ transit

■ pedestrian mezzanine level

SECOND STREET

A NEW OFFICE CENTER

The cluster principle has been examined at the scale of the Region, the Manhattan central business district, Midtown and Forty-Second Street. Now we look at a single cluster of office towers, a unified grove of Access Trees growing from the same root systems.

This is a demonstration of urban design principles that would work in many different places. We have set the demonstration west of Eighth Avenue because the survey of buildable land points to this area as a good location from the viewpoint of central business district activities. Needs of the existing residential community have not been analyzed except to find that there would be relatively little disruption of existing housing and that the new development would reverse physical deterioration going on around the waterfront by stimulating new residential, commercial and recreation investment there. In fact, clear designation of a location for office expansion on the West Side could stabilize existing uses whose sites are not needed for offices and ancillary activities, whereas they may now seem in danger of being swallowed up by the unplanned drift of office construction.

A new office cluster could divert the gradual creep westward of office buildings already threatening to overpower the theater district and cover much of Midtown with an undifferentiated "slab city."

Functional characteristics

The new center would be predominantly for office activities. Access would be patterned after the Grand Central Terminal area, though its focal point would be the intersection of two technologically new regional rapid transit lines, as shown in the cross section on pages 103-109.

Its design would provide for:
1. Pedestrian separation from vehicular movement at points of highest density.
2. Maximum use of modern technology to move people and goods.
3. Maximum use of industrialized building technology and environmental controls.
4. Careful comparison of alternative paths of movement to favor the largest number of people.
5. Easy access to utility lines and pipes, with provision for expansion and change.
6. Twenty-four hours of activity in the area.

For aesthetic goals, its design would provide:

Aesthetic characteristics

1. An imageable and coherent whole as seen from outside and felt from inside: a silhouette, for example, that is sharply differentiated from the surrounding area. In built-up areas of existing cities, this may be difficult, and it has a lower priority than other design goals; but it is worthwhile to aim at it.
2. Highly visible and expressive entry points on all major movement paths, below ground level as well as at grade.
3. A consistent visual vocabulary for all communication, including direction signs, transportation information and commercial signs.
4. A set of public spaces responsive to human density requirements.
5. Continuity with local urban design and architectural style where discernible and reasonable.
6. Maximum use and retention of major man-made landmarks.

photo by Jeremiah O. Bragstad

A NEW OFFICE CLUSTER

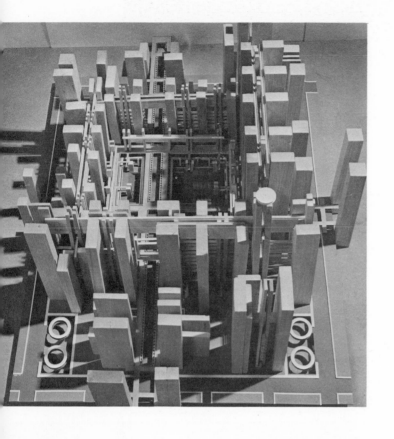

OFFICE CLUSTER MODEL

This model of a West Midtown Center provides 32 million square feet of office space, at a floor area ratio of 20:1. The area tested in the model is made up of 10 blocks which are 200' X 800' each, or 160,000 thousand square feet per block, excluding streets and sidewalks.

The net rentable office space would accommodate 120,000 office workers at an average of 200 square feet per person. This theoretical office cluster would be about as large as three Rockefeller Centers or three World Trade Centers.

The model portrays integration of developed spaces and the movement systems which serve the spaces. Ancillary service facilities would be located at the mezzanine and lower levels or at selected floors in the office towers above at which there are connections to other buildings in the cluster. Offices would constitute the great bulk of enclosed spaces. Conceivably, housing could occupy the top levels with good light and view and would provide twenty-four hour life to the center.

The plenum shown in the model as a major public plaza is the mixing interchange plane where all modes of travel meet. It is penetrated by each movement system and so provides a clear perception of each system and maximizes the ease of transfer among modes.

The main public space is slightly to the north, and the buildings on the south edge of the plaza are slightly lower to allow direct sunlight to reach it.

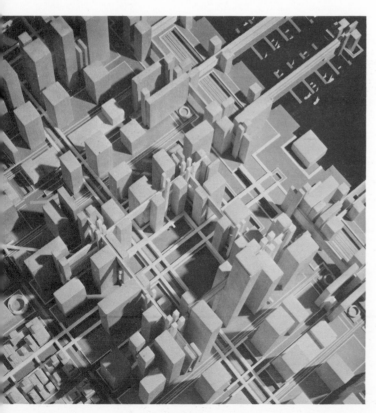

photos by Jeremiah O. Bragstad

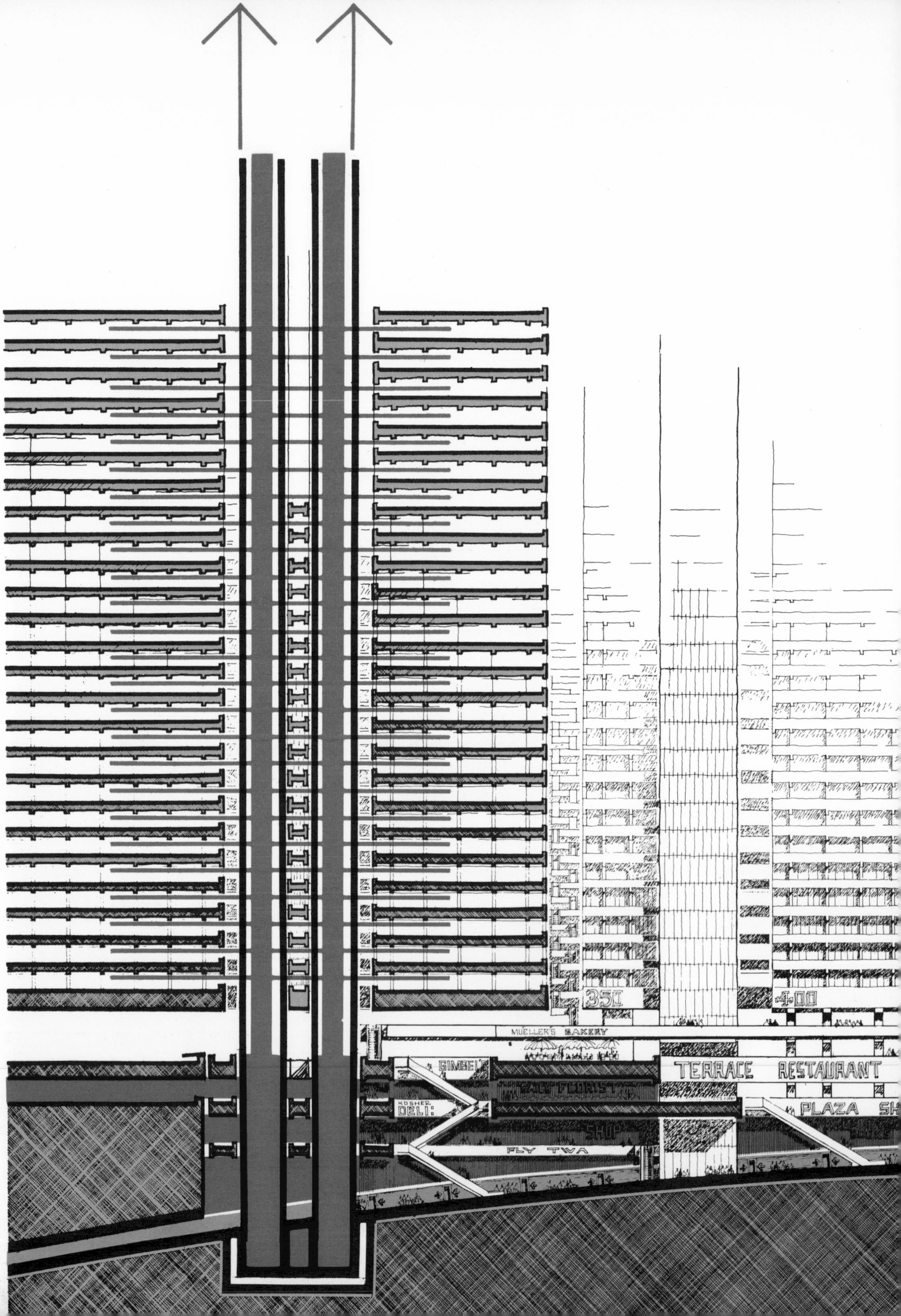

APPLICATION OF THE ACCESS TREE PRINCIPLE

This section through a theoretical new office cluster once again illustrates the integration of horizontal and vertical movement systems. The special station characteristics of trains using gravity and vacuum forces were tested in the design, hence the convex profile of the station.
The strongest control of design should be exercised at the levels just below and just above grade where almost everyone entering the cluster will move toward his individual destination or to another mode of transportation.

vertical movement — elevators

horizontal movement — public transit

A NEW OFFICE CLUSTER

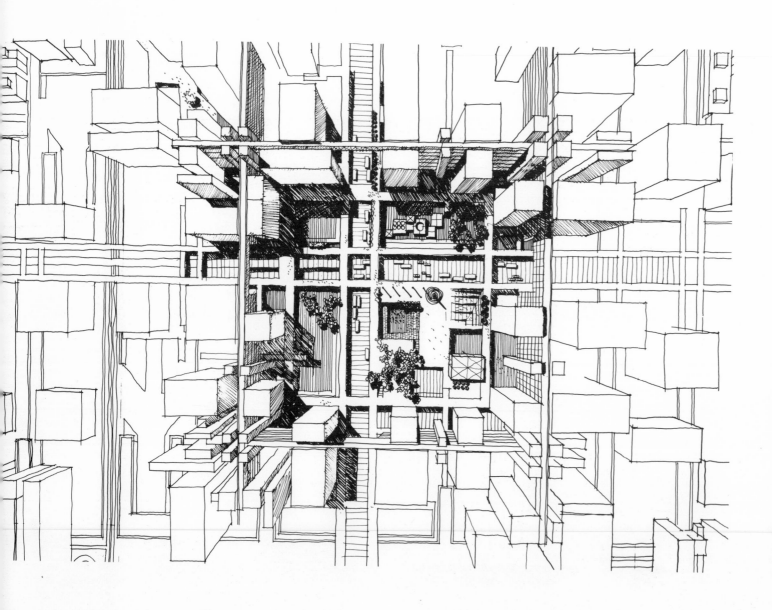

OFFICE CLUSTER SKETCHES

These perspective sketches help convey the spatial characteristics of the hypothetical office cluster. Residences have been incorporated in the cluster at the upper levels for the light, air and view. Residents in the cluster insure 24-hour use of the service activities, such as restaurants, meeting rooms, drug stores, delicatessens, etc.

"Sky walks" between buildings are studied here at different levels, such as every tenth floor, to provide flexibility in expanding horizontally as well as vertically.

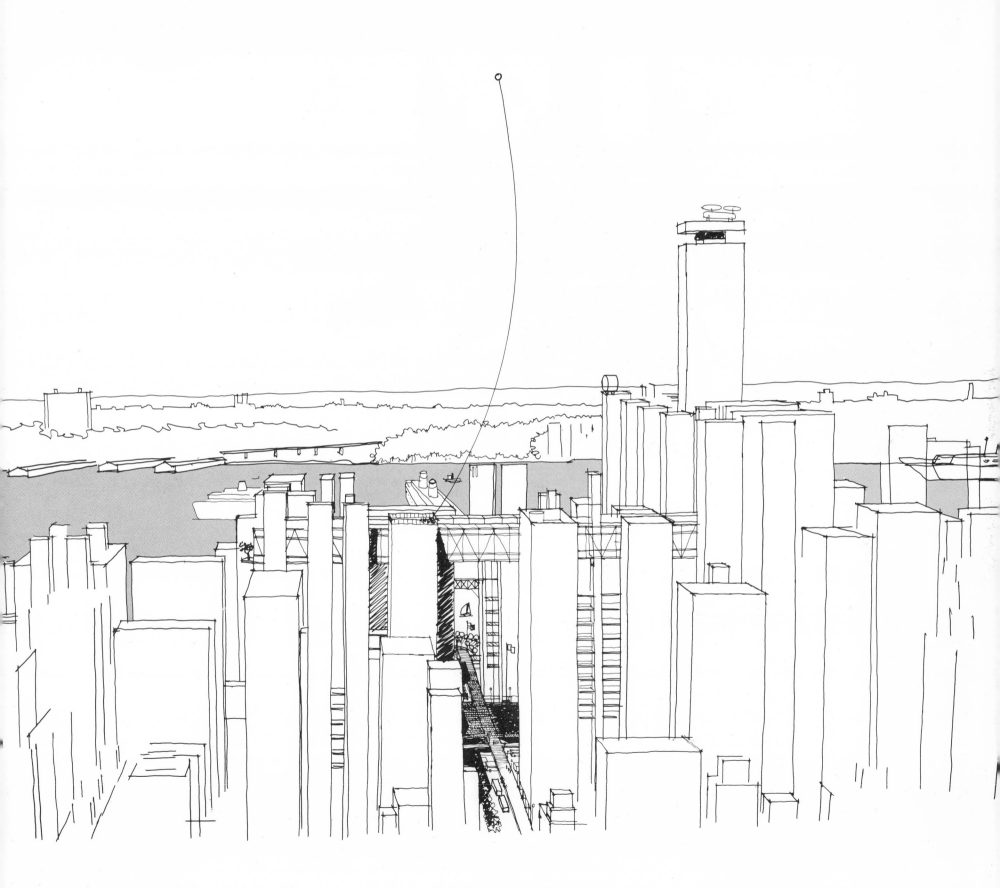

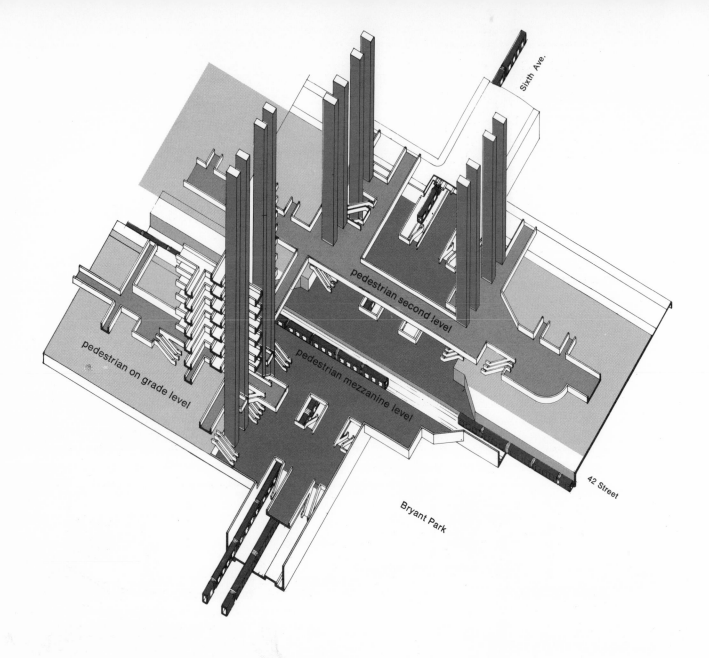

Sixth Ave.

pedestrian second level

pedestrian on grade level

pedestrian mezzanine level

42 Street

Bryant Park

SMALLER SCALE AMENITY

The subways

As the illustration of a typical journey to work shows in Chapter 2, the architecture of Manhattan subways is deplorable. In addition to a general need to improve maintenance, lighting and ventilation, the daily trip of the millions who depend on the subway could be made more pleasant by executing some of the following improvements:

Opening to light and air. New construction and the renovation of old buildings provide opportunities to open the below-grade portions of the subways to light and air from spaces associated with the circulation to and from adjacent buildings. The general principle consists simply of constructing a plaza at mezzanine level (halfway between the subway and the street) which would serve as a direct entrance to both the building and the subway. Openings to the sky from the mezza-

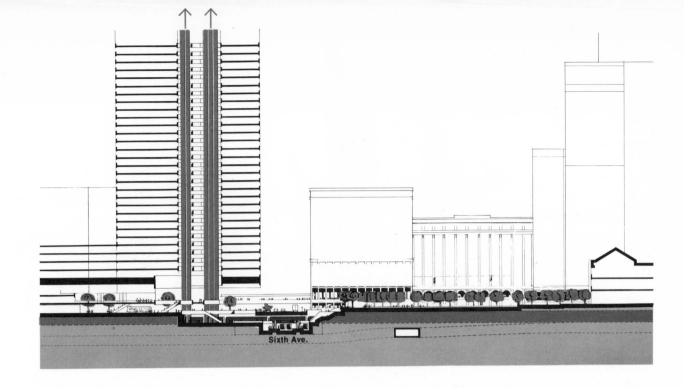

FORTY-SECOND STREET AND SIXTH AVENUE

The Access Tree principle is applied here at the intersection of the Sixth Avenue and Flushing line subways. Potential new office activity and retailing would have direct elevator service to subway mezzanines and platforms. New environmental amenity in the form of sunlight, visual clarity and proper ventilation would be introduced into the subway mezzanine area by opening it along the western edge of Bryant Park. Improved orientation to the park and station would be additional results.

Because of the resulting high pedestrian densities, grade-separated paths are shown for safety, convenience and walking-scale enjoyment.

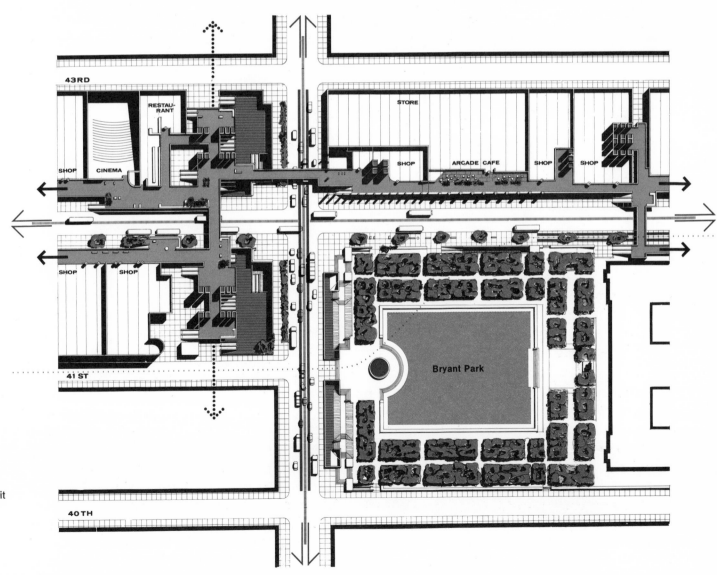

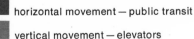

horizontal movement — public transit

vertical movement — elevators

pedestrian second level

pedestrian mezzanine level

THE ACCESS TREE AT BRYANT PARK

nine level could be fit into the street level without disrupting movement there if carefully designed, and the sunlight and fresh air would give a sense of openness to the subway level as well as to the mezzanine.

Employees in the connected buildings would benefit from the convenience of direct subway access to their offices, and subway riders would receive a visual amenity which also would identify the place as well as help clarify orientation.

Reorganization of circulation. Extensive widening of paths, increased ceiling heights, and a simplification of patterns and directional changes are the most essential tasks in reorganizing the underground environment. Such reorganization should relate below-ground circulation with above-ground destinations and circulation. Sidewalk widenings, street closings and improved building entries are integral parts of subway improvement.

Information and direction systems. While the circulation path should "explain itself," there will still be a need for supplementary information regarding the subway system. Since signs for commercial enterprises in subway concourses and platforms will probably persist, there is a primary need to establish locational priorities and performance standards to resolve the visual "noise" which prevents critical transit information from being read.

Priority in location, size, color, choice of lettering and method of illumination should be accorded transit signs. Their graphic form should be consistent and repetitive to quickly es-

tablish familiarity even in the stranger's eye and mind. Wherever possible, similar pieces of information should be displayed in the same relative position along paths.

Streets and other public places

Millions of people will still move over public rights-of-way on the surface. In addition to multiple level circulation to free the pedestrian, a special streets program could include relatively simple improvements, including:

Sidewalk widening. A casual survey of peak-hour pedestrian movements reveals a need for wider sidewalks in key areas, such as near Grand Central, near the Port Authority Bus Terminal and at the major shopping frontages. In certain cases, such widenings would represent a reversal of recent trends toward more space for cars and less for pedestrians. This should be possible if we divert traffic via crosstown tunnels, organize traffic according to different street classifications and provide better mass transportation service.

Boulevarding. Major east-west and north-south streets such as 34th, 42nd, 48th and 57th Streets and Fifth Avenue could be upgraded by a range of improvements including wider sidewalks, special paving, distinctive lights suited to the pedestrians, benches, standard and specimen trees, water displays and outdoor urban art. Litter disposal baskets, information and communication kiosks and balanced public-private signing should also be designed to give identity to these streets. Shelter structures for surface transit passengers should be provided for inclement weather protection.

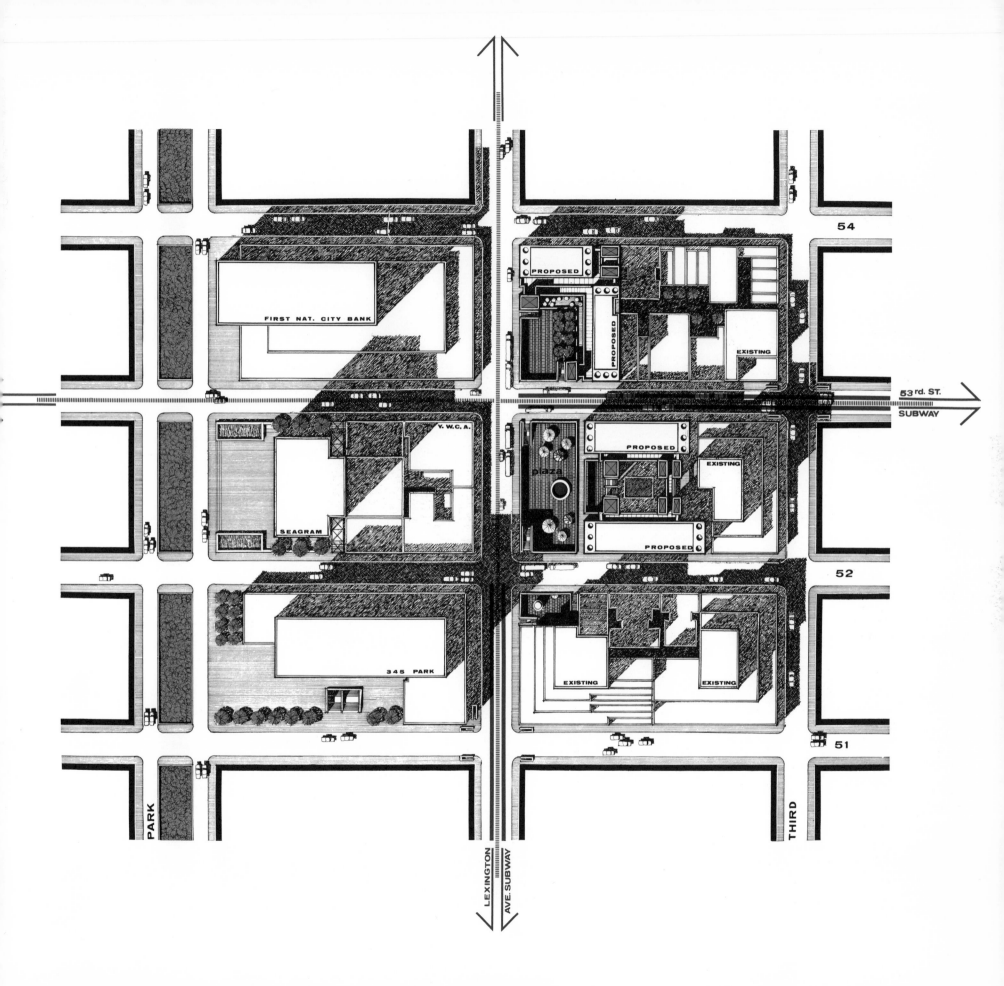

THE ACCESS TREE AT 51 AND 53 STREETS

SUBWAY LIGHT WELL AT FORTY-SECOND STREET AND EIGHTH AVENUE

The photograph and sketch at left indicate the dramatic increase in amenity if the Eighth Avenue mezzanine at Forty-Second Street were opened to light and air by means of a sunken plaza in front of the proposed Port Authority Bus Terminal extension.

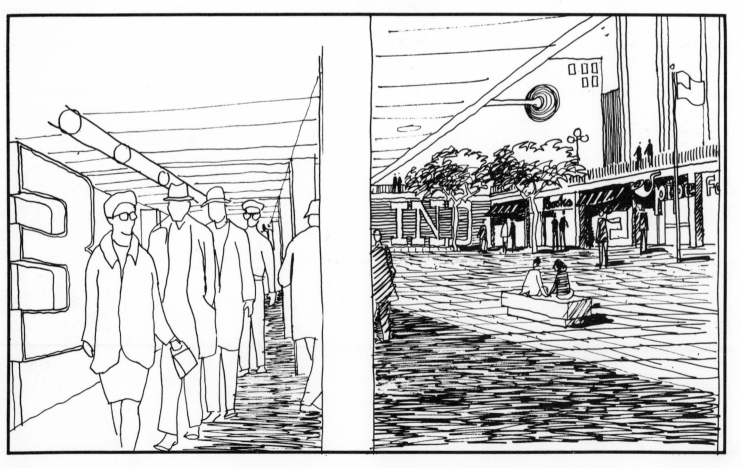

TIMES SQUARE
(right)

There are many possibilities for improving pedestrian ways at street level, e.g., by converting present vehicular routes to pedestrian use, widening sidewalks or cutting new walkways through built-up areas.

One such opportunity is in the very dense Times Square area. Depending on traffic improvements which divert some traffic from the area, such as crosstown tunnels, Broadway could be closed to vehicles between 59th and 23rd Streets. Broadway is particularly suited to exclusive pedestrian use because its diagonal direction confuses traffic movement and because it is not paired with a northbound avenue. On the other hand, this portion of Broadway is a favorite place for strolling, night and day, as well as a busy place for people walking to a destination.

VIEW OF TIMES SQUARE

HISTORIC PRESERVATION

The historic and cultural heritage of the City must be not only saved from demolition but incorporated into future development proposals. This preservation of landmark buildings and districts is imperative to bond the present with the past, thereby forming a continuity which will compliment the old while we build for the future.

Ironically, precisely because of its concentration of wealth, New York so far has been much more reckless in destroying its architectural heritage than many other cities.

Renewed emphasis must be placed on historic districts and not just landmark buildings. The Greenwich Village district, the theater district, the cast iron loft districts, as well as some of the early groups of office buildings, must be understood in their totality and not seen as merely individual buildings. Furthermore, some districts are not blessed with individual landmark buildings. Yet, as a whole, they make up distinctive historic entities in the City. Though the City's pioneering Landmark Preservation law gives a modicum of protection to the most valuable buildings, a broader use of other development controls is essential, as indicated in the next chapter. The use of incentive zoning for historic preservation, the transfer of zoning rights to nearby sites, and public assistance in the assembly of alternate sites can be among the possible tools.

JEFFERSON MARKET LIBRARY
Formerly the Jefferson Market Courthouse, at Sixth Avenue and 10th Street, by Vaux and Withers, 1876, restored by Giorgio Cavaglieri, 1967.

Saved from destruction through the efforts of Stanley B. Tankel and the Greenwich Village community, this landmark could be preserved because a new use was found for it: the former courthouse was converted into a public library. Death often comes to old structures because a new purpose, other than appearance, cannot be found for them even with a subsidy.

The subsidy, in this case, was considerable: the City paid $1,100,000 for the remodeling, or $50 per square foot. A standard new building providing for the same number of books and seats could be built at half the price. Of course, it would have provided neither the spaciousness nor the image of the old structure: on a per-cubic-foot basis, the cost was $1.89, compared to about $3.00 for a modern building.

The drawing at the far right shows the first train trip on the Sixth Avenue Elevated, April 29, 1878, with the Jefferson Market Courthouse in the background.

HAUGHWOUT BUILDING
(far left)

by J. P. Gaynor, iron by James Bogardus, 1857, Broadway at Broome Street. Located in the path of the future Lower Manhattan Expressway, one of the numerous distinctive buildings in the cast iron district, termed by the AIA "a highpoint in commercial architectural history." Most of the cast iron buildings are in a poor condition and have survived only because of lack of demand for new building sites in the "valley" between Midtown and downtown. As such demand develops, the cast iron facades of those buildings that cannot be preserved intact should be disassembled, saved, and re-constructed at a new site as part of a large-scale, coordinated development.

THE PLAZA HOTEL
(above left)

by Henry Janeway Hardenbergh, 1907, Fifth Ave. and Central Park South. Recently given a modicum of protection by reduction of the building bulk permissible on the site by zoning law.

HENRY VILLARD HOUSE
(below left)

by McKim, Mead & White, 1882-1886, 1909; also Babb, Cook & Willard. Madison Avenue between 50th and 51st Streets. These Italian Renaissance style mansions, housing the offices of Random House and the Roman Catholic Archdiocese of New York, are threatened with destruction, which would obliterate from that part of Madison Avenue the last trace of New York's turn-of-the century richness. Allowing the preservation of low buildings such as these to be counted as a floor-area bonus for adjacent sky-scrapers under the zoning law could make the preservation of these and similar landmarks economically feasible.

THE FLATIRON BUILDING
(right)

by D. H. Burnham & Company, 1902, at Fifth Avenue and 23d Street. With its unusual shape and rich details, one of the most memorable buildings in Manhattan.

5. IMPLEMENTATION

INTRODUCTION

Urban design is a relatively new term to express a concept which is as old as city building itself. Essentially, it is the relating of installations to each other in the urban setting which surrounds them. This report is concerned with the aspects of urban design which deal with buildings and the linkages between them; the open space around buildings and the transportation facilities which provide access to them. Just as it requires a number of professional disciplines to create an urban design plan, so its accomplishment involves many public agencies and private interests.

The opportunity for good urban design

Despite the investment of billions of dollars in Manhattan's central business district since the beginning of the subway-skyscraper era, only once every thirty years have groups of buildings been created in which principles of urban design are recognizable. These are the Grand Central complex, Rockefeller Center and the World Trade Center. Each of these projects is atypical in that it involved New York's rarest phenomenon, a large tract of land developed by a single entrepreneur.

Clearly, therefore, well-designed business districts with good access to buildings from subways and a better environment for the pedestrian generally will not be carried out with business-and-government-as-usual.

The time is ripe for change, however. In the first place, we have every reason to believe there will be tremendous investments, both private (for profit) and public (for service) in New York's business districts in Manhattan, in Brooklyn and Jamaica.

The advent of State responsibility for subway and railroad improvement through the new Metropolitan Transportation Authority is a major event in the City's history.

In the next two decades, close to $1 billion is proposed to be spent on public transportation improvement in the Manhattan central business district from State, City and federal funds now in hand or in sight. More will be needed and surely will be made available.

Matching this investment in central business district accessibility will be private capital investment in office buildings and related structures of from $3 billion to $4 billion in 1968 dollars.

In Manhattan's prime central business areas there is ample profit for private developers to enable them to "build it right," especially if building regulations which raise costs in the name of better urban design can also provide offsetting increases in income.

On the public side, there is ample personal satisfaction and political glory for those who become identified with ending public squalor in the paths of daily travel for literally millions of New Yorkers.

Moreover, it is now universally recognized that public and private investment in central business districts are directly related to one another. This is especially obvious as regards public investment in subway and railroad facilities without which high density business districts could never rise.

It follows, therefore, that there is a direct public interest in insisting that private developments tie in with public facilities. This happens also to be highly advantageous for the private investor in the long run. As a result, regulations to insure that private developments are built in harmony with public streets and transportation facilities have long been justified under the inherent right of the government to protect the public interest against private acts which impair the health, safety, and general welfare of society.

The findings of this report redefine in terms of urban design the harmony which should and could be the goal of public administration and public regulation of private development. These are not "revolutionary" proposals. They call for no more than evolutionary changes from business-as-usual along familiar constitutional and administrative paths.

Obstacles to good urban design

To say that it is possible to change building practices in New York's central business districts without amending the United States Constitution or suffering a political revolution does not imply that the task will be easy. Let us examine some of our major difficulties.

1. Large-scale land assemblage is impracticable without power of condemnation. With some few exceptions on the edges of central business districts, there are no single fee holdings in them of more than a single block in area. Even single block ownership is a rarity. The opportunity for private enterprise to assemble a site suitable for another Grand Central or Rockefeller Center does not exist. The bargaining power of "holdouts" has collapsed many projects at even the single building scale.

So serious is the holdout game that a New York developer has suggested that as land becomes more scarce at locations best served by transportation, the public has an interest in breaking the holdout's grip. As quoted in the May 17, 1964 New York **Times,** a prominent developer suggested:

The City Planning Commission could issue a certificate stating that a site assembled and ready for improvement is being blocked by a small parcel, for example, less than 10 percent of the total area. If the small parcel is not itself suitable for improvement, the city could then be authorized to acquire the property for 150 percent of the appraised value and sell it at that price to the developer.

Nothing more was heard of this proposal, which has obvious administrative and constitutional pitfalls. Yet, the suggestion may anticipate things to come. Perhaps at some future date urban design planning will define so precisely the public interest in strategically located large-scale developments that a taking with fair compensation will be justified. Perhaps the concept of urban renewal, where condemnation powers are justified by the public interest in improving blighted areas, will be extended by redefinition of what constitutes "blight."

As the City extends its subways and underground pedestrian ways, opportunities to acquire key sites will arise. Montreal, for example, has acquired and is holding land at subway stations for future development.

For the foreseeable future, however, we shall have to live with the fact that private initiative by itself will rarely be able to assemble central business

SINGER BUILDING LOBBY
(right)
The lobby of the 47-story Singer Building at 149 Broadway, completed in 1908 by Ernest Flagg as a pioneering structure in modern architectural design (and for a while the world's tallest skyscraper) was one of the City's most magnificent indoor pedestrian spaces. It was demolished in 1968, to make way for the U.S. Steel office building. Across the street from it, a nondescript block of buildings was torn down to make room for a plaza for the U.S. Steel building, while another adjacent block of nondescript buildings (on small parcels, hence difficult to assemble) will remain intact. The placement of the new office tower on either one of the adjacent, esthetically valueless blocks would have saved the historic Singer Building and its neighbor, at 165 Broadway, likewise with an elegant lobby and a distinctive spiral staircase. But, the City lacked the legal machinery to allow the Singer Building to be counted in lieu of a plaza for the U.S. Steel Building, or to assemble the alternate site for U.S. Steel in the public interest. Nor was the public sufficiently aroused about the destruction of a unique part of the national heritage.

photo by Louis B. Schlivek

district building sites of more than a few acres.

2. Decision-making is secretive. Because of the competitive nature of the real estate business generally and the "holdout" problem in particular, private developments in central business districts are carried on under a cloak of secrecy.

Even public agencies with unquestioned powers of eminent domain often prefer to acquire land by voluntary sale for reasons of economy and public relations.

Secrecy can be devastating to planning and cooperation between developers, both private and public.

3. Decision-making is scattered. The essence of private enterprise is competitive, separate decision-making. Co-operation between adjacent owners is sometimes good business, but generally each developer thinks in terms of his own property by itself.

Public agencies operating in New York have been quite as self-centered over the years as private entrepreneurs. It is not just the early private transit entrepreneurs who first built elevated lines and subways in squalid isolation from the city structure they served. The Transit Authority has, in general, continued this tradition, a notable exception being the subway station in its own building at Jay Street, Brooklyn. One need not single out the Transit Authority to make this point. The highway building authorities have rarely tied in with any other developments. In short, the functional walls between public agencies are no less formidable than profit-motive walls. Sometimes it seems as though state and city agencies and private developers each had built-in compulsions to brutalize a given piece of urban fabric, such as we find at today's Times and Herald

Squares. These "paper" walls between agencies, both public and private, result in real walls detouring subway riders from their destinations, blocking pedestrians from light and air and cutting meaningful open space into a patchwork.

4. Action outstrips urban design planning. Once a site is assembled and financing is obtained, the private developer is in a race with time to meet his money-flow problems. Taxes and interest do not wait. Under the restraints of secrecy, it is not surprising that he does not wish to reveal his plans to public agencies until they have matured. Then he is a man in a great hurry with little leeway to coordinate his development with public or other private developments outside the four corners of his building site.

The public agency is also compelled to either make final plans in a hurry (which means unilaterally) or, even worse, to refuse to update old engineering plans made in hopes of future authorizations.

5. Good urban design usually increases costs as well as benefits. The principles stated in this report call for a number of facilities used without charge such as pedestrian ways and escalators. They may be worth the price in increased rents and greater public convenience, but the price is higher.

To do things right often takes design and negotiating time. Such time is expensive to private developers without rent rolls and to public officials who eye their rising costs of wages and materials. Public agencies no less than private developers are conscious of added continuing costs, such as public maintenance and police protection.

Private developers, therefore, must find compensating revenue for income lost on low-profit uses such as shops and eating places, not to mention outright amenities with out-of-pocket expenses. Of course, there is recognition of the fact that some amenities do increase income and that rents upstairs are not unrelated to conditions below. Thus, Rockefeller Center maintains the cleanliness of its subway mezzanine, City Investing Company voluntarily improved its subway exit when renovating its building and the Bowery Savings Bank contributed to an escalator leading to its main office.

In fact, during the postwar years, private enterprise has generally built to better standards than most hard-pressed public agencies have been allowed to. This has been especially true of City agencies. The Transit Authority's plans to rebuild the disgraceful 42nd Street Shuttle, for example, has been regularly vetoed over the years.

One reason for official penny-pinching is that no agency adds up the total costs and total benefits of urban design. Sometimes the cheapest program for the agencies making a decision is the most expensive for the public as a whole if all construction and infrastructure costs are included. If the value of time saved by pedestrians is added to the equation, the benefits of good design even more outweigh the costs. Highway builders determine the utility and priority of proposed roads on the basis of the capitalized value of time saved by its construction. In urban design, this value is never considered. Yet, opportunities abound in the Manhattan central business district to produce tremendous benefits in time saved for a comparatively low investment. And time saved is only one of the significant factors.

One recent and surely classic failure of urban design illustrates the opera-

The wall of a subway station is exposed during excavation for an office building at 32 Street and Park Avenue. Instead of being demolished to open the station to light and air, the wall is being carefully underpinned and preserved. A parallel, private wall will rise next to it, precluding the possibility of opening the station at that site for another half century. While this book was being written, a dozen such opportunities for opening subway stations were lost in the CBD. Only at two sites were tentative moves toward open linkages with transit stations made. While the Transit Authority now has a program for improving station appearance by means of new tile, lighting and signs, it has no program for the structural alterations needed.

tion of each of the foregoing five factors. This is the development of the Avenue of the Americas from 50th Street to 57th Street which might have been a brilliant extension of the spirit of Rockefeller Center. It now seems incredible that the Transit Authority excavated what amounted to a mezzanine over the Sixth Avenue subway tracks while extending the subway north — and then filled it with earth instead of pedestrians and shoppers. Contemporaneously, great new office buildings plus a major hotel were built on the Avenue, each isolated from the other and from Rockefeller Center. Lost was a great opportunity to create a mezzanine shopping and service street under the Avenue to link all the new office buildings and the hotel to each other and to Rockefeller Center. Such an underground street could have redressed the loss of small shops, inexpensive eating places and service establishments which seldom are included in corporate headquarters or hotels.

Here all five factors were at work: the many sites with many owners, the secretive decision-making, the lack of communication between private developers and the Transit Authority, the stale plans for the subway and the unwillingness of the private developers to go to the expense of changing plans. Despite some unheeded yells from concerned spectators, the opportunity was lost among the players like an infield fly.

No one player could be charged with the error and in this fact, perhaps, lies the hope that none of the five factors is an insuperable block to better urban design.

To sum up, we find that good urban design will not occur under present building practices; that public intervention in private building operations is justified; that such intervention must not destroy profit-motive incentives; and that public agencies must work more effectively together and with private builders toward urban design goals.

The recommendations that follow are based on this reasoning. They are also designed to mitigate the five factors identified above which frustrate better urban design in central business districts.

RECOMMENDATIONS

To implement the findings of this report, we make the following recommendations which relate not only to Midtown Manhattan, but to New York's other major business districts.

1. Central business district planning

New York's Department of City Planning should undertake a new dimension of planning for each of the City's central business districts, especially Midtown Manhattan where a great volume of private and public building activity is about to take place.

We shall describe in two parts this new level of planning which operates much closer to the ground than the City's Planning Commission has generally heretofore worked. In practice, they would be one continuous operation.

(a) Central business district plans

A central business district plan requires studies for each district to identify its boundaries based on economic growth projections and transportation potentials, to establish how the district performs its functions, what its space requirements and its urban design goals are, what public improvements are scheduled for it and what further public improvement it will need.

A central business district plan would be the basis of a rezoning of the district in a manner much more closely tailored to its best potential than is the case in any of the City's major central business districts today. The public improvement elements of such plans would carry current two-dimensional route and capital budget descriptions to three-dimensional design concepts in selected areas.

The second purpose of such a major business district plan is to engender public discussion and to alert both private developers and public agency chiefs to what the City expects of them in each district's foreseeable future.

The problems arising from small building sites, secrecy and scattered decision-making could be largely overcome as zoning controls tailored to specific ends known to all took effect and public agencies knew better what was expected of them in three-dimensional terms.

(b) Urban design programs

However, a district plan in sufficient detail to form the basis of improved zoning and to serve as a guide to public improvements will not, of itself, lead to the realities of good urban design.

Also needed is an urban design staff within the Department of City Planning in readiness to conceive, present, and negotiate opportunities in urban design in the relatively short period of grace allowed by our system of city building between the moment a decision is made to go forward with a development and the time the specific blueprints are locked up. The small urban design staff recently established in the Department of City Planning as the result of the recommendations of the Paley Commission is a start in this direction. It should be enlarged by as many architect-planner personnel as each business district plan may require.

The purpose of the urban design staff is to give New York the capability to anticipate or at least to react in time to real estate and public improvement events, to bring key people together at moments of design decision, and to replace stale and (unimaginative) plans with fresh and more comprehensive conceptions. In smaller cities such as Philadelphia, Toronto or Montreal, this role can be played by a skillful and talented planning director. New York, that metropolitan giant with two central business clusters — Midtown and Downtown Manhattan — larger than Chicago's loop district and others of major city size, such as downtown Brooklyn and Jamaica, should organize its urban design capability at a matching scale.

We recognize, of course, that just as such business district plans would set objectives for urban design programs, so the district plans would be tailored by the City Planning Commission to its city-wide master plan objectives.

2. Development coordination

Central business district plans, revised zoning, and a strong staff with ongoing design capability will not of themselves achieve urban design success. Administrative machinery is needed to see that public improvements carry out the plans, and to nudge private enterprise toward desired design standards. We call this machinery development or construction coordination — a euphemism for the power to successfully negotiate needed public and private action at the right time and place and in the best possible manner.

To identify the need for development coordination power is one thing. To locate this power is another.

The public improvement programs which affect the building of New York's central business districts, of which subway and railroad projects are but the most obvious, are carried out by many City and State agencies. Some of the most powerful agencies, such as the Metropolitan Transportation Authority, its subsidiary Transit Authority, the State Development Corporation, the Port of New York Authority and even the City's own Housing and Redevelopment Board are relatively independent of either the Governor or the Mayor. As the balance between what might be called Mayor-power, Governor-power and Authority-power is continually shifting, we offer no precise formula for business district development coordination machinery. The decision as to just how to set up what is needed must be made by the Governor and the Mayor in a contemporary context of contending political power centers.

We do, however, suggest that the City could make the first move on the first central business district plan by designating a development coordinator for the district reporting to the Chairman of the City Planning Commission. Such a district development coordinator would work continuously in a single district with its planning staff. He would get to know his district's needs, private investors and civic groups intimately. He would work there through every available channel, and expedite such approvals as may be required from the Mayor, the City Planning Commission, the Board of Estimate, the City Council and the various authorities. He would thus help a multiplicity of developers to move as though the defined center were under a single responsible ownership. He could overcome many of the difficulties cited above in the existing New York approach to urban design in the developing central business districts. New York has already made a start in this direction in the recently organized Office of Lower Manhattan Development.

3. A Mid-Manhattan Association

When a central business district suffers from stagnation, obsolescence or creeping blight, business leadership responds by forming a civic association. The results are often spectacular, as in the case of downtown Pittsburgh, Baltimore and lower Manhattan. In New York, the Downtown-Lower Manhattan Association, the Downtown Brooklyn Development Committee and the Greater Jamaica Development Corporation are examples of citizens' organizations formed to suggest and promote plans to stimulate new growth.

Midtown Manhattan has no such district-wide organization, due perhaps to its continuous dynamic growth for the past fifty years and to the fact that its business leadership has been organized along north-south or east-west linear lines in organizations such as the Fifth Avenue Association, Avenue of the Americas Association, Broadway

Association and West Side Association of Commerce, Forty-Second Street Property Owners' Association and Thirty-Fourth Street Midtown Association.

Midtown Manhattan, as this report shows, is no longer a series of parallel ribbons of development along north-south avenues or east-west streets. It is a rectangular area with interplay of business activities in every direction of the compass. To maintain its dynamism, the nation's largest central business district needs a civic association which is dedicated to the area as a whole. Such an organization would supplement, not duplicate, the existing Avenue Associations, just as Regional Plan Association relates to the Passaic Valley Citizens Planning Association, Mid-Hudson Pattern for Progress, or New York's City-wide Commerce and Industry Association and Economic Development Council.

A Mid-Manhattan Association built on a broad base of business, civic and professional leadership could contribute immeasurably to a central business district plan for Midtown, and to drafting the zoning revisions flowing from it. It could be a key factor in the construction coordinator's continuing negotiations with private developers and public agencies required to build the future Midtown Manhattan to its fullest potential.

Midtown Manhattan is the only major central business cluster in the nation, as far as we can ascertain, which does not have a business and civic organization which speaks for the district as a whole.

4. Incentive zoning

There could be brilliant urban design plans for Midtown Manhattan coordi-

Shown here are two of the few sunken plazas in Manhattan actually built: in front of the General Motors building at Fifth Avenue and 59th street (above), and in front of the J. C. Penney building on Sixth Avenue (below). The first greatly enriches the space of the Grand Army Plaza, which it faces, but fails to connect to the BMT subway station a block away, to which it could have given some light, air and orientation. The walls between the plaza and the subway station symbolize the institutional barriers between individual builders and public agencies.

The plaza in front of the Penney building also has no connection to the nearby subway.

nated with future subway and other improvements and yet under the economic incentives of present zoning regulations the desired results would not be achievable.

Many of the urban design recommendations of this report run counter to what we have called "business-as-usual" private development practices which are building slab city with great rapidity. Under current zoning regulations, a sometimes meaningless plaza unused by pedestrians enables the developer to gain a bonus of floor area ratio while an essential underground pedestrian way connecting directly to the subway is not constructed because it goes unrewarded. For example, the 345 Park Avenue Building plaza (just south of the Seagram Building) is probably less useful than an underground connection to the Lexington Avenue subway would have been. The former was rewarded by a floor area ratio bonus. The latter would have added to costs without gaining rent income benefits.

The Zoning Resolution hems in the architect-urban designer because the economics of permitted building configurations dictate their form in ways which may or may not enhance their environment. Uniform plaza setbacks in front of slab city office buildings are as monotonously predictable as the old-law wedding cake setbacks.

San Francisco has recently enacted central business district zoning regulations which are based on the same principle as New York's plaza-bonus but, like New York's new theater-bonus, are aimed at more meaningful ends, including subway access and other urban design features suited to that West Coast city.

In its basic terms, the San Francisco

photo by Louis B. Schlivek

ordinance permits a minimum floor area ratio in a given downtown commercial district which, while not confiscatory, is less than most developers would prefer. Bonuses in floor area ratio are then offered the developer under stated and measurable standards. These features for which a rentable floor area bonus is given are summarized in **San Francisco Zoning Study** (1966) as follows:

1. Good access to the building, and improvement of access to other properties in the area, from the various means of transportation feeding the downtown area.
2. Improvement of pedestrian movement into the building, along the street and between streets.
3. Provision of pedestrian amenity by means of ground level open space.
4. Arrangement of the building so as to provide light and air to streets.
5. Protection and enhancement of views.

Under these purposes, most bonus features provided by the developer could be expected to be found at one of three locations: either at ground level around the base of the building, just above or below ground level where movement of persons could be facilitated without the use of streets, or at upper levels where there would be certain effects upon the shape of the building. In some cases, also, a premium might be awarded based on the location of the new building, since locations with the best accessibility may be appropriate for higher intensities of development.

The San Francisco bonus features (not all of which are necessarily applicable to New York City and some of which are in effect in New York's Zoning Resolution now) include floor area bonuses for rapid transit access directly from the site to a subway mezzanine, rapid transit proximity for sites other than those with direct rapid transit access, parking access as a direct pedestrian link from the building to a parking structure, multiple building entrances, sidewalk widening inside the property line, shortening walking distance from one public street to another by way of a plaza, arcade or passageway, plazas for public amenity, a side setback for light and air, low coverage of upper floors, view protection features and observation decks.

Incentive zoning points the way to a means of clearing the most difficult hurdle in better city building — the increase in private costs necessary to achieve general benefits. Admittedly, no regulations based on measurable (and therefore somewhat rigid) standards can give the architect the flexibility of a large site and a single owner such as Grand Central, Rockefeller Center or the World Trade Center. But when incentive zoning is based on achieving the goals of a central business district plan, it gives great promise as a way to reward good urban design with added rentable floor space. San Francisco's bonus system, designed among other goals to encourage developers to give open spaces to speed pedestrian movement and provide sitting places for office workers, is a long step forward from New York's pioneering plaza bonus which assumes that any open space on the street level is **per se** a good thing.

Incentive zoning should prove useful in any situation where greater intensity of use than the reasonable minimum is justified by the business district plan and urban design goals. Thus, if contemporary office building sterilizes the street scene and desiccates the environment by eliminating specialty shops, service establishments, and small restaurants, as is the case on today's Park and Third Avenues and the Avenue of the Americas, the roof of a single story commercial building dedicated to such uses could constitute the basis of a "roof plaza" bonus possibly combined with a sidewalk widening. Alternatively, basement space or a subway mezzanine devoted to such uses might also justify a floor area ratio bonus. A variant of this principle which preserves corporate identity without sucking the blood of the street scene is illustrated by the new General Motor's building at 59th Street and Fifth Avenue where shops and restaurants line a sunken plaza on the Avenue.

These examples are given as illustrations of the possibilities of the bonus principle. Before any bonus is written into the zoning law, a thorough analysis should be made of its economic feasibility and consequences and whether it will encourage the goals of the district plan.

Related to incentive zoning is the assignment of air rights over one building to increase the floor area ratio of an adjacent building. Such combinations are especially valuable in preserving low, landmark structures such, for example, as the former Villard Mansion at Madison Avenue and 50th Street. They can also be used to pay back some of the capital costs of public plazas either at or below grade which should be created by the kind of subway improvements recommended in this report (see page 78).

5. Underground pedestrian ways

New York already has an important system of underground pedestrian ways in the form of subway mezzanines and private ways such as the heavily traveled, but dismal passage from Pennsylvania Station to Herald Square (see map at page 66).

One of the recommendations of this report is that these underground streets should be greatly improved, opened where possible to light and air, and extended to give access both to building lobbies and to shops and other commercial uses carried on below street level as at Grand Central Station and Rockefeller Center today.

To require underground pedestrian ways from subway mezzanines into abutting buildings (and beyond) is analogous to requiring land developers to dedicate public access roads from the municipal street. Each new building which abuts a subway mezzanine should be required to provide or dedicate access walkways into its premises under reasonable standards administered by the Planning Commission.

To make this new requirement palatable and wholly fair and to increase clustering with amenity at subway stations, we suggest a floor area ratio bonus related to the square footage of private property given up to such pedestrian ways in building.

In order to obtain a continuity of underground pedestrian ways, we suggest that an official map should be prepared for each central business district similar to an official map of streets. Such an official map of underground ways would undoubtedly have extended the Avenue of the Americas mezzanine north from 50th Street to 57th Street. Each new building could have been required to tie into this pedestrian way. The disappointment described above of recent developments in this area would have been avoided.

The question of mapping pedestrian ways so that they will pass under buildings which connect directly with subway mezzanines or platforms and connect with buildings more remote from the subway deserves detailed study. Practical problems of location of underground utilities, foundations and lot lines must be considered before any "paper streets" are laid down across private property. Presumably these pedestrian ways through private property would remain as private streets maintained and regulated by the owners of the buildings above them. However, it is not inconceivable that some main shopping and pedestrian underground streets might be dedicated to and policed and maintained by public authority as subway mezzanines are today.

From the standpoint of urban design, it should be recognized that each subway station from the Times or Herald Squares' scale to a local stop has a character of its own. The official map of pedestrian ways might include relatively small reservations for light wells, assuming, of course, that a floor area ratio bonus for such sunken "plazas" is in effect. More ambitious opportunities for sunken plazas on the scale of Rockefeller Center's skating rink, for example, should be part of a central business district plan rather than an official map.

Since the effect of an official mapping across private property is, to some degree, the taking of property, this recommendation should be evolved with the full understanding and, if possible, the cooperation of affected property owners.

An official map of present and proposed public underground pedestrian ways under public property presents no legal difficulties. A regulation that new developments be required to tie into such ways would seem to be entirely reasonable.

The Transit Authority does not have a clear policy, or an effective apparatus to encourage new development to integrate with its elaborate pedestrian concourses. In most cases due to long delays and expensive legal agreements, new development is discouraged from integrating with the existing systems. This process should be reversed by speeding the technical and legal procedures as well as providing floor area ratio bonuses to pay the extra cost incurred by the private developer. This needed interaction of the public and private sector could, in the future, provide new amenity and safety in the city.

6. Taxation

A vital and growing central business district such as Midtown Manhattan, which is not in need of urban renewal aids to stimulate private investment, needs no special tax privileges. If nodes of higher density development are desired at nodes of public transportation, some adjustment upwards of land assessments relative to building assessments might be considered as a lever to promote such development.

On the other hand, there should be no real estate tax penalty enforced on a property owner who chooses to enhance a national or international reputation by building to the highest standards of architectural design, including voluntarily reducing floor area ratio in order to enhance the beauty of a building or to make it stand out from its neighbors.

Commercial office buildings are generally valued for real estate tax purposes by capitalization of net income. What a building can "throw off" is its measure of worth to investor and tax assessor alike. The Seagram Building at Park Avenue and 52nd Street, however, cost more than a business-as-usual building. It is taxed at a higher valuation than its rent roll measure would indicate. Joseph E. Seagram and Sons took their case to New York's Court of Appeals and lost by a decision which has had various interpretations, most of which tend to limit the applicability of the case to its particular facts.

The Seagram doctrine, however, hangs like a cloud over the construction of meaningful and magnificent structures in New York City. Even lesser evidence of civic-minded building might attract the tax assessor's eye.

The courts did not make clear just what extra value in the Seagram Building is being taxed. No objective standards or tests are stated. There is no way a taxpayer can protect himself against such ambiguity except to build with inconspicuous mediocrity.

If we are to have more monumental and magnificent structures in New York, then, it would seem advisable for the legislature to establish statutory criteria for office building assessment to assure corporate sponsors of aesthetics that they will not be penalized.

While high real estate burdens may not be a decisive influence in many corporate decisions, there is no sense in stacking the cards **against** good design.

Summary

In sum, these recommendations urge metropolitan New York City to deal with its central business districts in the manner smaller cities deal with theirs. They constitute a program for city planning at the city scale. In terms of commercial floor space, transportation and economic activity, no city in the United States has as large a central business district as either mid-Manhattan or lower Manhattan. A few cities can match the scale of a downtown Brooklyn or a Jamaica center. New York's secondary business centers, such as Fordham Road or Flushing, each serve the equivalent of a major city elsewhere.

New York is both a 300-square mile, 5-county area and a cluster of interrelated but distinct central business districts. Each of these districts requires the planning, construction coordination and civic concern of a Philadelphia, a San Francisco or a Toronto. This report will merely add to the literature of urban design unless New York overcomes its giantism and moves ahead on a more human and three-dimensional scale.

The problem of urban redesign of New York is not primarily the lack of imaginative designs or of architects, engineers and planners who are each eager to make their ideas known. Every school of architecture and planning, and every internationally known urban designer is ready to take over. What is lacking is a practical method of harnessing the unrivalled vitality of private developers and investors to form teams which are big enough to work with the City and the authorities and thus to concert their energies to create the new composite centers which are now called for. To this end New York City cannot follow the approaches of old world cities and the socialist cultures without destroying her unique dynamism; but New York can achieve rational and beautiful urban redesign to meet the highest standards of the modern age by moving along the lines indicated in this book.

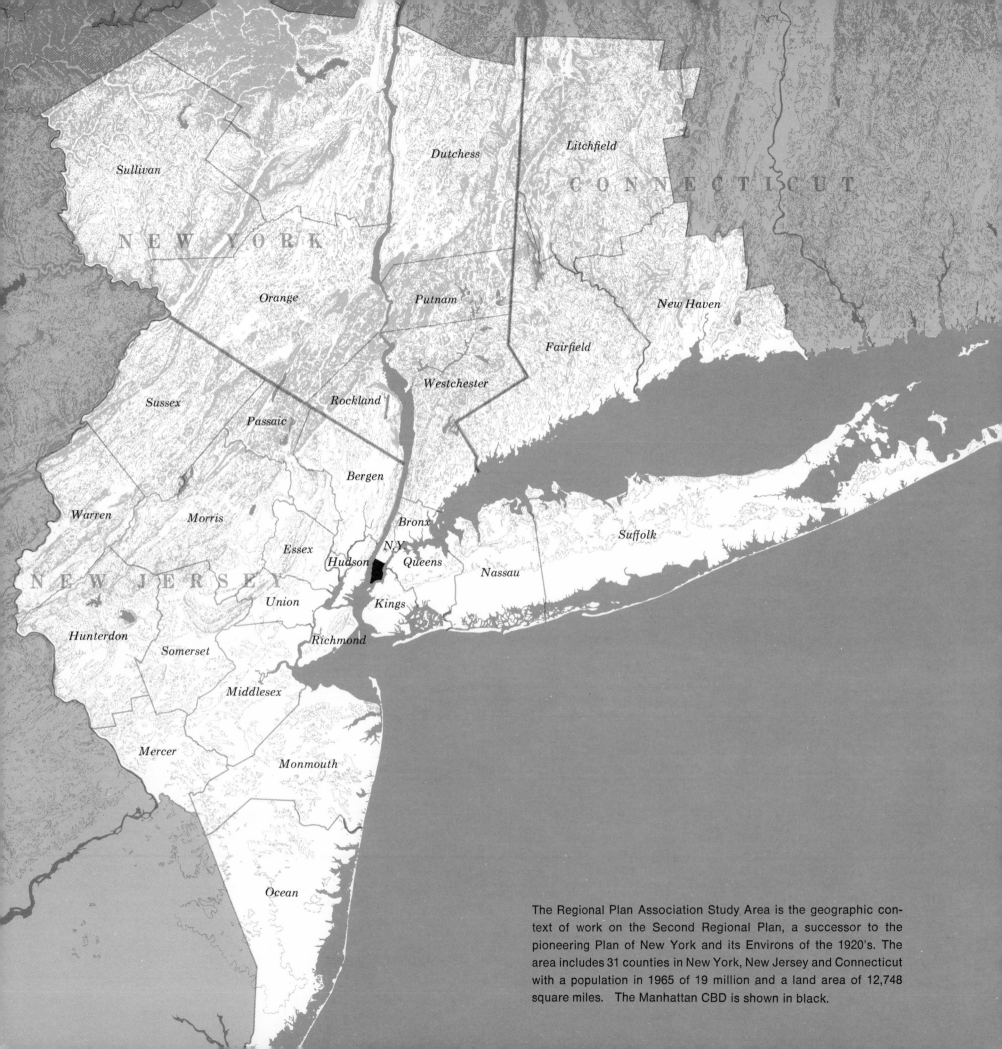

Sullivan

NEW YORK

Orange

Dutchess

Litchfield

CONNECTICUT

Putnam

New Haven

Fairfield

Westchester

Sussex

Rockland

Passaic

Warren

Morris

Bergen

Essex

Hudson

Bronx

N.Y.

Queens

Suffolk

NEW JERSEY

Union

Nassau

Hunterdon

Somerset

Richmond

Kings

Middlesex

Mercer

Monmouth

Ocean

The Regional Plan Association Study Area is the geographic context of work on the Second Regional Plan, a successor to the pioneering Plan of New York and its Environs of the 1920's. The area includes 31 counties in New York, New Jersey and Connecticut with a population in 1965 of 19 million and a land area of 12,748 square miles. The Manhattan CBD is shown in black.

INDEX